# What the World Rejected: Hitler's Peace Offers 1933–1940

By Dr. Friedrich Stieve

Ostara Publications

What the World Rejected: Hitler's Peace Offers 1933–1940
By Dr. Friedrich Stieve
First published 1940

Ostara Publications
http://ostarapublications.com

ISBN 978-1-68418-610-5

# Contents

# List of Illustrations

# Part I: What the World Rejected: Hitler's Peace Offers 1933–1940

## Section 1: Introduction

Dr. Friedrich Stieve was Germany's foremost diplomatic historian of the first half of the twentieth century. Before the First World War Stieve wrote a book of poems (1908) and a biography of the mediaeval Italian prince Ezzelino da Romano (1909).

Stieve began writing history in 1916 with the work *Schwedische Stimmen zum Weltkrieg*. This was followed by *Die Politischen Probleme Des Weltkrieges;* and in 1918 with *Studien zur Weltkrise.*

In 1920, he published *Gedanken über Deutschland*, a reflection on Germany's political and social conditions of the time. In 1924 he published *Iswolski und der Weltkrieg*, and in 1934, produced a comprehensive history of the German nation, *Geschichte des deutschen Volkes.*

In 1936, he published *Abriß der deutschen Geschichte 1792–1933*.

During the National-Socialist period, Stieve produced the 1939 pictorial book *Neues Deutschland* (with photographs supplied by Hitler's personal photographer, Heinrich Hoffmann), indicative of his support for the new order.

He continued his output, and later works included the 1940 *Politische Gespräche*, the 1941 *Wendepunkte europäischer Geschichte vom Dreißigjährigen Krieg bis zur Gegenwart,* the 1942 *Deutschlands europäische Sendung im Laufe der Jahrhunderte,* the 1943 *Deutsche Tat für Europa,* and in 1943, the overview *Elfhundert Jahre Vertrag von Verdun,* a lecture delivered to the Preußischen Akademie der Wissenschaften.

*What the World Rejected: Hitler's Peace Offers 1933–1940* was first published as an essay in Berlin in 1940 in German as *Was die Welt nicht wollte: Hitlers Friedensangebote 1933–1939.*

Within the year, it had been translated and distributed in French, Spanish, and English, with the latter version (from which the text contained herein is taken) being published in 1940, by the *Washington Journal,* a now long defunct magazine based in Washington DC.

## Section 2: Hitler's Peace Offers 1933–1940 by Dr. Friedrich Stieve

Germany's enemies maintain today that Adolf Hitler is the greatest disturber of peace known to history, that he threatens every nation with sudden attack and oppression, that he has created a terrible war machine in order to cause trouble and devastation all around him.

At the same time they intentionally conceal an all-important fact: they themselves drove the Leader of the German people finally to draw the sword. They themselves compelled him to seek to obtain at last by the use of force that which he had been striving to gain by persuasion from the beginning: the security of his country.

They did this not only by declaring war on him on September 3, 1939, but also by blocking step by step for seven years the path to any peaceful discussion.

The attempts repeatedly made by Adolf Hitler to induce the governments of other states to collaborate with him in a reconstruction of Europe represent an ever-recurring pattern in his conduct since the commencement of his labors for the German Reich.

But these attempts were wrecked every time by reason of the fact that nowhere was there any willingness to give them due consideration, because the evil spirit of the Great War still prevailed everywhere, because in London and Paris and in the capitals of the Western Powers' vassal states there was only one fixed intention: to perpetuate the power of Versailles.

FRIEDRICH STIEVE

# Was die Welt nicht wollte

Hitlers Friedensangebote 1933 – 1939

ZENTRALVERLAG DER NSDAP., FRANZ EHER NACHF. GMBH., BERLIN

Herausgegeben von der Deutschen Informationsstelle

***Front page of the original German edition*** **Was die Welt nicht wollte, *Berlin, 1940.***

A rapid glance at the most important events will furnish incontrovertible proof for this statement.

When Adolf Hitler came to the fore, Germany was as gagged and as helpless as the victors of 1918 wanted her to be. Completely disarmed, with an army of only 100,000 men intended solely for police duties within the country, she found herself within a tightly closed ring of neighbors all armed to the teeth and leagued together.

To the old enemies in the West, Britain, Belgium, and France, new ones were artificially created and added in the East and the South: above all Poland and Czechoslovakia.

A quarter of the population of Germany was forcibly torn away from their mother country and handed over to foreign powers. The Reich, mutilated on all sides and robbed of every means of defense, at any moment could become the helpless victim of some rapacious neighbor.

Then it was that Adolf Hitler for the first time made his appeal to the common sense of the other powers.

On May 17, 1933, a few months after his appointment to the office of Reichskanzler, he delivered a speech in the German Reichstag, from which we extract the following passages:

> Germany will be perfectly ready to disband her entire military establishment and destroy the small amount of arms remaining to her, if the neighboring countries will do the same thing with equal thoroughness.
>
> . . . Germany is entirely ready to renounce aggressive weapons of every sort if the armed nations, on their part, will destroy their aggressive weapons within a specified period, and if their use is forbidden by an international convention.
>
> . . . Germany is at all times prepared to renounce aggressive weapons if the rest of the world does the same. Germany is prepared to agree to any solemn pact of non-aggression because she does not think of attacking anybody but only of acquiring security.

No answer was received. Without paying any heed the others

continued to fill their arsenals with weapons, to pile up their stores of explosives, to increase the numbers of their troops.

At the same time the League of Nations, the instrument of the victorious powers, declared that Germany must first pass through a period of "probation" before it would be possible to discuss with her the question of the disarmament of the other countries.

On October 14, 1933, Hitler broke away from this League of Nations with which it was impossible to come to any agreement.

Shortly afterwards, however, on December 18, 1933, he came forward with a new proposal for the improvement of international relations. This proposal included the following six points:

> 1. Germany receives full equality of rights.
> 2. The fully armed States undertake amongst themselves not to increase their armaments beyond their present level.
> 3. Germany adheres to this agreement, freely undertaking to make only so much actual moderate use of the equality of rights granted to her as will not represent a threat to the security of any other European power.
> 4. All States recognize certain obligations in regard to conducting war on humane principles, or to the elimination of certain weapons for use against the civilian population.
> 5. All States accept a uniform general control which will watch over and ensure the observance of these obligations.
> 6. The European nations guarantee one another the unconditional maintenance of peace by the conclusion of nonaggression pacts, to be renewed after ten years.

Following upon this a proposal was made to increase the strength of the German army to 300,000 men, corresponding to the strength required by Germany "having regard to the length of her frontiers and the size of the armies of her neighbors," in order to protect her threatened territory against attacks.

The defender of the principle of peaceable agreement was thus trying to accommodate himself to the unwillingness of the others to disarm by expressing a desire for a limited increase of armaments for his own country.

An exchange of notes, starting from this and continuing for years, finally came to a sudden end with an unequivocal "no" from France. This "no" was moreover accompanied by tremendous increases in the armed forces of France, Britain, and Russia.

In this way Germany's position became still worse than before. The danger to the Reich was so great that Adolf Hitler felt himself compelled to act.

On March 16, 1935, he reintroduced conscription. But in direct connection with this measure he once more announced an offer of agreements of an extensive nature, the purpose of which was to ensure that any future war would be conducted on humane principles, in fact to make such a war practically impossible by eliminating destructive armaments. In his speech of May 21, 1935, he declared:

> The German Government is ready to take an active part in all efforts which may lead to a practical limitation of armaments.
>
> It regards a return to the former idea of the Geneva Red Cross Convention as the only possible way to achieve this. It believes that at first there will be only the possibility of a gradual abolition and outlawry of weapons and methods of warfare which are essentially contrary to the Geneva Red Cross Convention which is still valid.
>
> Just as the use of dumdum bullets was once forbidden and, on the whole, thereby prevented in practice, so the use of other definite arms should be forbidden and prevented.
>
> Here the German Government has in mind all those arms which bring death and destruction not

so much to the fighting soldiers as to non-combatant women and children.

The German Government considers as erroneous and ineffective the idea to do away with aeroplanes while leaving the question of bombing open. But it believes it possible to proscribe the use of certain arms as contrary to international law and to excommunicate those nations which still use them from the community of mankind—its rights and its laws.

It also believes that gradual progress is the best way to success. For example, there might be prohibition of the dropping of gas, incendiary and explosive bombs outside the real battle zone.

This limitation could then be extended to complete international outlawry of all bombing. But so long as bombing as such is permitted, any limitation of the number of bombing planes is questionable in view of the possibility of rapid substitution.

Should bombing as such be branded as a barbarity contrary to international law, the construction of bombing aeroplanes will soon be abandoned as superfluous and of no purpose.

If, through the Geneva Red Cross Convention, it turned out possible as a matter of fact to prevent the killing of a defenseless wounded man or prisoner, it ought to be equally possible to forbid, by an analogous convention, and finally to stop, the bombing of equally defenseless civilian populations.

In such a fundamental way of dealing with the problem, Germany sees a greater reassurance and security for the nations than in all pacts of assistance and military conventions.

The German Government is ready to agree to any limitation which leads to abolition of the heaviest arms, especially suited for aggression. Such are, first, the heaviest artillery, and secondly, the heaviest tanks. In view of the enormous fortifications on the

> French frontier such an international abolition of the heaviest weapons of attack would ipso facto give France 100 percent security.
>
> Germany declares herself ready to agree to any limitation whatsoever of the caliber-strength of artillery, battleships, cruisers, and torpedo boats.
>
> In like manner the German Government is ready to accept any international limitation of the size of warships. And finally it is ready to agree to limitation of tonnage for submarines, or to their complete abolition in case of international agreement.
>
> And it gives further assurance that it will agree to any international limitations or abolition of arms whatsoever for a uniform space of time.

This time again Hitler's declarations did not find the slightest response.

On the contrary, France made an alliance with Russia in order to increase her preponderating influence on the Continent still further, and to augment to a gigantic degree the pressure on Germany from the East.

In view of the evident destructive intentions of his opponents, Adolf Hitler was therefore obliged to take new measures to ensure the safety of the German Reich.

On March 3, 1936, he occupied the Rhineland, which had been without military protection since Versailles, and thus closed the wide gate through which the Western neighbor could carry out an invasion.

Once again he followed the defensive step which he had been obliged to take with a liberal appeal for general reconciliation and for the settlement of all differences. On March 31, 1936, he formulated the following peace plan:

> 1. In order to give to future agreements securing the peace of Europe the character of inviolable treaties, those nations participating in the negotiations do so only on an entirely equal footing and as equally esteemed members.

The sole compelling reason for signing these treaties can only lie in the generally recognized and obvious practicability of these agreements for the peace of Europe, and thus for the social happiness and economic prosperity of the nations.

2. In order to shorten in the economic interest of the European nations the period of uncertainty, the German Government proposes a limit of four months for the first period up to the signing of the pacts of non-aggression guaranteeing the peace of Europe.

3. The German Government gives the assurance not to add any reinforcements whatsoever to the troops in the Rhineland during this period, always provided that the Belgian and French Governments act in the same way.

4. The German Government gives the assurance not to move during this period closer to the Belgian and French frontiers the troops at present stationed in the Rhineland.

5. The German Government proposes the setting up of a commission composed of the two guarantor Powers, Britain and Italy, and a disinterested third

***German troops cross the Rhine, 1936.***

neutral power, to guarantee this assurance to be given by both parties.

6. Germany, Belgium, and France are each entitled to send a representative to this Commission. If Germany, France, or Belgium think that for any particular reason they can point to a change in the military situation having taken place within this period of four months, they have the right to inform the Guarantee Commission of their observations.

7. Germany, Belgium, and France declare their willingness in such a case to permit this Commission to make the necessary investigations through the British and Italian military attaches, and to report thereon to the Powers participating.

8. Germany, Belgium and France give the assurance that they will bestow the fullest consideration to the objections arising therefrom.

9. Moreover the German Government is willing on a basis of complete reciprocity with Germany's two western neighbors to agree to any military limitations on the German western frontier.

10. Germany, Belgium, and France and the two guarantor Powers agree to enter into negotiations under the leadership of the British Government at once or, at the latest, after the French elections, for the conclusion of a 25-years non-aggression or security pact between France and Belgium on the one hand, and Germany on the other.

11. Germany agrees that Britain and Italy shall sign this security pact as guarantor Powers once more.

12. Should special engagements to render military assistance arise as a result of these security agreements, Germany on her part declares her willingness to enter into such engagements.

13. The German Government hereby repeats its proposal for the conclusion of an air-pact to supplement and consolidate these security agreements.

14. The German Government repeats that should the Netherlands so desire it is willing to include that country too in this West-European security agreement.

15. In order to stamp this peace-pact, voluntarily entered into between Germany and France, as the reconciliatory conclusion of a centuries-old dispute, Germany and France pledge themselves to take steps to see that in the education of the young, as well as in the press and publications of both nations, everything shall be avoided which might be calculated to poison the relationship between the two peoples, whether it be a derogatory or contemptuous attitude, or improper interference in the internal affairs of the other country. They agree to set up at the headquarters of the League of Nations at Geneva, a joint commission whose function it shall be to lay all complaints received before the two governments for information and investigation.

16. In pursuance of their intention to give this agreement the character of a sacred pledge, Germany and France undertake to ratify it by means of a plebiscite if the two nations.

17. Germany expresses her willingness, on her part, to establish contact with the states on her south-eastern and north-eastern frontiers, in order to invite them directly to conclude the pacts of non-aggression already proposed.

18. Germany expresses her willingness to re-enter the League of Nations, either at once, or after the conclusion of these agreements.

At the same time, the German Government again expresses as its expectation that, after a reasonable time and by the method of friendly negotiations, the question of colonial equality of rights and that of the separation of the Covenant of the League of Nations from its foundations in the Versailles Treaty will be cleared up.

19. Germany proposes the setting up of an International Court of Arbitration, which shall be responsible for the observance of the various agreements and whose decisions shall be binding on all parties.

After the conclusion of this great work of securing European peace, the German Government considers it urgently to endeavor by practical measures to put a stop to the unlimited competition in armaments. In her opinion this would mean not merely an improvement in the financial and economic positions of the nations, but above all a diminution of the psychological tension.

The German Government, however, has no faith in the attempt to bring about universal settlements, as this would be doomed to failure from the outset, and can therefore be proposed only by those who have no interest in achieving practical results.

On the other hand it is of the opinion that the negotiations held and the results achieved in limiting naval armaments should have an instructive and stimulating effect.

The German Government therefore proposes that future conferences shall have one clearly defined objective.

For the present, it believes the most important task is to bring aerial warfare into the moral and humane atmosphere of the protection afforded to non-combatants or the wounded by the Geneva Convention.

Just as the killing of defenseless wounded, or prisoners, or the use of dumdum bullets, or the waging of submarine warfare without warning, have been either forbidden or regulated by international conventions, so it must be possible for civilized humanity to prevent the senseless abuse of any new type of weapon, without running counter to the object of warfare.

The German Government therefore puts forward the proposal that the immediate practical tasks of this conference shall be:

1. Prohibition of dropping gas, poison, or incendiary bombs.

2. Prohibition of dropping bombs of any kind whatsoever on open towns and villages outside the range of the medium-heavy artillery of the fighting fronts.

3. Prohibition of the bombarding with long-range guns of towns more than 20 km. distant from the battle zone.

4. Abolition and prohibition of the construction of tanks of the heaviest type.

5. Abolition and prohibition of artillery of the heaviest calibre.

As soon as possibilities for further limitation of armaments emerge from such discussions and agreements, they should be utilized.

The German Government hereby declares itself prepared to join in every such settlement, in so far as it is valid internationally. The German Government believes that if even a first step is made on the road to disarmament, this will be of enormous importance to the relationship between the nations, and to the recovery of confidence, trade, and prosperity.

In accordance with the general desire for the restoration of favorable economic conditions, the German Government is prepared immediately after the conclusion of the political treaties to enter into an exchange of opinions on economic problems with the other nations concerned, in the spirit of the proposals made, and to do all that lies in its power to improve the economic situation in Europe, and the world economic situation which is closely bound up with it.

The German Government believes that with the peace plan proposed above it has made its

> contribution to the reconstruction of a new Europe on the basis of reciprocal respect and confidence between sovereign states. Many opportunities for such a pacification of Europe, for which Germany has so often in the last few years made her proposals, have been neglected. May this attempt to achieve European understanding succeed at last!
>
> The German Government confidently believes that it has opened the way in this direction by submitting the above peace plan.

Anyone who today reads this comprehensive peace plan will realize in what direction the development of Europe, according to the wishes of Adolf Hitler, should really have proceeded. Here was the possibility of truly constructive work, this could have been a real turning-point for the welfare of all nations. But once more he who alone called for peace was not heard. Only Britain replied with a rather scornful questionnaire which avoided any serious consideration of the essential points involved.

Incidentally, however, she disclosed her actual intentions by setting herself up as the protector of France and by instituting and commencing regular military staff conversations with the French Republic just as in the period before the Great War.

There could no longer be any doubt now that the Western Powers were following the old path towards an armed conflict and were steadily preparing a new blow against Germany, although Adolf Hitler's whole thoughts and endeavors were directed towards proving to them that he wanted to remain on the best possible terms with them.

In the course of the years he had undertaken numerous steps in this direction, of which a few more shall be referred to here. He negotiated the Naval Agreement of June 18, 1935, with Great Britain, which provided that the German Navy should have a strength of 35% of that of the British Navy.

By this he wanted to demonstrate that the Reich, to use his own words, had "neither the intention nor the means, nor was it necessary" to enter into any rivalry as regards naval power, such as had had so fateful an influence on its relations to Great

Britain in the well-remembered days before the Great War.

He assured France on every possible occasion of his desire to live at peace with her. He repeatedly renounced in plain terms any claim to Alsace-Lorraine. On the return to the Reich of the Saar territory as the result of the plebiscite, he declared on March 1, 1935:

> It is our hope that through this act of just compensation, in which we see a return to natural reason, relations between Germany and France have permanently improved.
>
> Therefore as we desire peace, we must hope that our great neighbor is ready and willing to seek peace with us. It must be possible for two great peoples to join together and collaborate in opposing the difficulties which threaten to overwhelm Europe.

He even endeavored to arrive at a better understanding with Poland, the eastern ally of the Western Powers, although this country had unlawfully incorporated millions of Germans in 1919 and had subjected them to the worst oppression ever since.

On January 26, 1934, he concluded a non-aggression pact with her in which the two Governments agreed "to settle directly all questions of whatever sort which concern their mutual relations."

Thus on all sides he opposed to the enemy plans his determination to preserve peace and strove to protect Germany in this way. When however he saw that London and Paris were arming for an attack, he was once more obliged to undertake fresh measures of defense.

The enemy camp, as we have seen above, had been enormously extended through the alliance between France and Russia. In addition to this the two powers had secured a line of communication to the south of the Reich through Czechoslovakia having concluded a treaty with Russia which put her in the position of a bridge between east and west.

Czechoslovakia, however, was in control of the high-lying country of Bohemia and Moravia, which Bismarck had called

***The* Führerbau *in Munich, decked out with the French and British flags for the 1938 conference.***

***From left to right: Chamberlain, Daladier, Hitler, Mussolini, and Ciano pictured before signing the Munich Agreement.***

the citadel of Europe, and this citadel projected far into German territory. The threat to Germany thus assumed truly overpowering proportions.

The genius of Adolf Hitler found a way of meeting this danger. The conditions in German Austria, which under the terror of the Schuschnigg Government were tending towards civil war, offered him the opportunity of stepping in to save the situation, and to lead back into the Reich the sister nation to the south-east that had been sentenced by the victorious powers to lead the life of a hopelessly decaying "Free State."

After he had thus established himself near the line of communication between France and Russia mentioned above, a process of dissolution set in in the mixed state of Czechoslovakia, which had been artificially put together from the most diverse national elements, until after the liberation of the Sudetenland and the secession of Slovakia, the Czechs themselves asked for the protection of the German Reich.

With this the enemy's bridge came into Adolf Hitler's possession; and at the same time direct connection was made possible with Italy, whose friendship had been secured some time previously.

While he was gaining this strategic success for the security of his country, Adolf Hitler was again endeavoring with great eagerness to reach a peaceable understanding with the Western Powers.

In Munich directly after liberation of the Sudeten Germans, approved by Britain, France, and Italy, he made an agreement with the British Prime Minister, Neville Chamberlain, the text of which was as follows:

> We have had a further meeting to-day and have agreed in recognizing that the question of Anglo-German relations is of the first importance for the two countries and for Europe.
>
> We regard the agreement signed last night and the Anglo-German Naval Agreement as symbolic of the desire of our two peoples never to go to war with one another again.

> We are resolved that the method of consultation shall be the method adopted to deal with any other questions that may concern our two countries, and we are determined to continue our efforts to remove possible sources of difference and thus to contribute to assure the peace of Europe.
>
> September 30, 1938.
>
> Adolf Hitler, Neville Chamberlain.

Two months later, on Hitler's instructions, the German Foreign Minister, von Ribbentrop, made the following agreement with France:

> Herr Joachim von Ribbentrop, Reich Minister for Foreign Affairs, and M. Georges Bonnet, French Minister of Foreign Affairs, acting in the name and by the order of their Governments, are, at their meeting in Paris, on December 6, 1938, agreed as follows:
>
> 1. The German Government and the French Government fully share the conviction that peaceful and good-neighborly relations between Germany and France constitute one of the most essential elements for the consolidation of the situation in Europe and the maintenance of general peace.
>
> The two Governments will in consequence use all their efforts to ensure the development of the relations between their countries in this direction.
>
> 2. The two Governments recognize that between the two countries there is no territorial question outstanding, and they solemnly recognize as final the frontiers between their countries as they now exist
>
> 3. The two Governments are resolved, while leaving unaffected their particular relations with other Powers, to remain in contact with regard to all questions concerning their two countries, and mutually to consult should the later evolution of

those qualities lead to international difficulties.

In token whereof the representatives of the two Governments have signed the present Declaration, which comes into immediate effect.

Done in two original Documents in the French and German language respectively, in Paris, December 6, 1938.

Joachim von Ribbentrop,
Reich Minister for Foreign Affairs
Georges Bonnet,
Minister for Foreign Affairs.

According to all calculations one should have been able to assume that the way was clear for collaborative reconstruction in which all leading powers would participate, and that the Führer's endeavors to secure peace would at last meet with success.

But the contrary was true. Scarcely had Chamberlain reached home when he called for rearmament on a considerable scale and laid plans for a new and tremendous encirclement of Germany.

Britain now took over from France the leadership of this further encirclement of the Reich, in order to obtain a substitute for the lost Czechoslovakia many times its value. She opened negotiations with Russia, granted Poland a guarantee and also Rumania, Greece and Turkey. These were alarm signals of the greatest urgency.

Just at this time Adolf Hitler was occupied with the task of finally eliminating sources of friction with Poland.

For this purpose he had made an uncommonly generous proposal by which the purely German Free City of Danzig would return to the Reich, and a narrow passage through the Polish Corridor, which since 1919 had torn asunder the north-eastern part of Germany to an unbearable extent, would provide communication with the separated area.

This proposal, which moreover afforded Poland the prospect of a 25-year nonaggression pact and other advantages, was nevertheless rejected in Warsaw, because there it was believed, conscious as the authorities were of forming one of the principal members of the common front set up by London against Germany, that any concession, however minor, could be refused.

This was not all! With the same consciousness Poland then started to be aggressive, threatened Danzig, and prepared to take up arms against Germany.

Thus the moment was close at hand for the attack on the Reich by the countries which had been brought together for the purpose. Adolf Hitler, making a final extreme effort in the interests of peace, saved what he could.

On August 23rd, Ribbentrop succeeded in reaching an agreement in Moscow for a non-aggression pact with Russia. Two days later the German Führer himself made a final and truly remarkable offer to Britain, declaring himself ready "to enter into agreements with Great Britain", "which... would not only, on the German side, in any case safeguard the existence of the British Empire, but if necessary would guarantee German assistance for the British Empire, irrespective of where such assistance might be required."

At the same time he was prepared "to accept a reasonable limitation of armaments, in accordance with the new political situation and economic requirements".

And finally he assured once again that he had no interest in the issues in the west and that "a correction of the borders in the west are out of any consideration."

The reply to this was a pact of assistance signed the same day between Britain and Poland, which rendered the outbreak of war inevitable.

Then a decision was made in Warsaw to mobilize at once against Germany, and the Poles began with violent attacks not only on the Germans in Poland, who for some time had been the victims of frightful massacres, but on Germans in German territory.

But even when Britain and France had already declared war, as they intended, and Germany had overcome the Polish danger in the east by a glorious campaign without a parallel, even then Adolf Hitler raised his voice once more in the name of peace.

He did so although his hands were now free to act against the enemy in the west. He did so, although the fight against him personally was proclaimed in London and Paris, in immeasurable hate, as a crusade.

At this moment he possessed the supreme self-control to proclaim in his speech of October 6, 1939, a new plan for the pacification of Europe to public opinion throughout the world. This plan was as follows:

> By far the most important task, in my opinion, is the creation of not only a belief in, but also a sense of, European security.
>
> 1. For this it is necessary that the aims of the foreign policy of each European State should be made perfectly clear.
>
> As far as Germany is concerned, the Reich Government is ready to give a thorough and exhaustive exposition of the aims of its foreign policy. In so doing, it begins by stating that the Treaty of Versailles is now regarded by it as obsolete, in other words, that the Government of the German Reich and with it the whole German people no longer see cause or reason for any further revision of the Treaty, apart from the demand for adequate colonial possessions justly due to the Reich, involving in the first place a return of the German colonies.
>
> This demand for colonies is based not only on Germany's historical claim to her colonies, but above all on her elementary right to a share of the world's resources of raw materials. This demand does not take the form of an ultimatum, nor is it a demand which is backed by force, but a demand based on political justice and sane economic principles.
>
> 2. The demand for a real revival of international economic life coupled with an extension of trade and commerce presupposes a reorganization of the international economic system, in other words, of production in the individual states.

***Adolf Hitler spells out a plan for peace in Europe, October 6, 1939.***

In order to facilitate the exchange of the goods thus produced, however, a new system of markets must be found and a final settlement of currencies arrived at, so that the obstacles in the way of unrestricted trade can be gradually removed.

3. The most important condition, however, for a real revival of economic life in and outside of Europe is the establishment of an unconditionally guaranteed peace and of a sense of security on the part of the individual nations.

This security will not only be rendered possible by the final sanctioning of the European status, but above all by the reduction of armaments to a reasonable and economically tolerable level.

An essential part of this necessary sense of security, however, is a clear definition of the legitimate use and application of certain modern armaments which can at any given moment strike straight at the heart of every nation and hence create a permanent sense of insecurity.

In my previous speeches in the Reichstag I made proposals with this end in view. At that time they were rejected - presumably for the simple reason that they were made by me.

I believe, however, that a sense of national security will not return to Europe until clear and binding international agreements have provided a comprehensive definition of the extent to which the use of certain weapons is permitted or forbidden.

The Geneva Convention once succeeded in prohibiting, in civilized countries at least, the killing of wounded, the ill-treatment of prisoners, war against noncombatants, etc., and just as it was possible gradually to achieve the universal observance of this statute, a way ought surely to be found to regulate aerial warfare, the use of poison gas, of submarines etc., and also so to define contraband that war will lose its terrible character of a conflict waged against women and children and against non-combatants in general.

The growing horror of certain methods of modern warfare will of its own accord lead to their abolition, and thus they will become obsolete.

In the war with Poland, I endeavored to restrict aerial warfare to objectives of military importance, or only to employ it to combat resistance at a given point.

But it must surely be possible to emulate the Red Cross in drawing up some universally valid international regulation.

It is only when this is achieved that peace can reign, particularly on our densely populated continent a peace which, un-contaminated by suspicion and fear, will provide the only possible condition for real economic prosperity.

I do not believe that there is any responsible statesman in Europe who does not in his heart desire prosperity for his people. But such a desire can only be realized if all the nations inhabiting this continent decide to work together.

To assist in ensuring this co-operation must be the aim of every man who is sincerely struggling for the future of his own people.

To achieve this great end, the leading nations on this continent will one day have to come together in order to draw up, accept and guarantee a statute on a comprehensive basis which will ensure for them a sense of security, of calm, in short, of peace.

Such a conference could not possibly be held without the most thorough preparation, i. e. without exact elucidation of every point at issue.

It is equally impossible that such a conference, which would determine the fate of this continent for many years to come, could carry on its deliberations while cannons are thundering, or mobilized armies bringing pressure to bear upon it. Since, however, these problems must be solved sooner or later, it would surely be more sensible to tackle the solution before millions of men are first uselessly sent to their death, and billions of dollars' worth of property destroyed.

The continuation of the present state of affairs in the west is unthinkable. Each day will soon demand increasing sacrifices.

Perhaps the day will come when France will begin to bombard and demolish Saarbrücken. The German artillery will in turn lay Mühlhausen in ruins. France will retaliate by bombarding Karlsruhe, and Germany in her turn shell Strassburg.

Then the French artillery will fire at Freiburg, and the Germans at Kolmar or Schlettstadt. Long-range artillery will then be set up, and from both sides destruction will strike deeper and deeper, and whatever cannot be reached by the long-range artillery will be destroyed from the air.

And that will be very interesting for certain international journalists, and very profitable for the aeroplane, arms, and munition manufacturers, etc., but appalling for the victims.

And this battle of destruction will not be confined to the land. No, it will reach far out over the sea. To-day there are no longer any islands.

And the national wealth of Europe will be scattered in the form of shells, and the vigor of every nation will be sapped on the battlefields.

One day, however, there will again be a frontier between Germany and France, but instead of flourishing towns there will be ruins and endless graveyards.

The fate of this plan was the same as that of all the previous appeals made by Adolf Hitler in the name of reason, in the interests of a true renascence of Europe.

His enemies paid him no heed.

On this occasion also no response was forthcoming from them. They rigidly adhered to the attitude which they had taken up in the beginning.

In the face of this series of historical facts is there any need for further details as to the question of why they did so? They had created Versailles, and when Versailles threatened to collapse they wanted the war, in order to follow it with an even worse Versailles.

The reproaches which they make today to Adolf Hitler and Germany, recoil one and all on those who make them, and characterize their actions.

They are the disturbers of peace, they are the ones who meditate the forcible oppression of other peoples and seek to plunge Europe in devastation and disaster.

If it were not so, they would long ago have taken the hand that was stretched out to them or at least have made a gesture of honestly wishing to cooperate in a new order, and thus spare the nations "blood, tears and sweat" in excess.

World history is the world court; and in this case as always when it reaches its decision it will pronounce a just verdict.

# Part II: An Appeal for Peace and Sanity, Adolf Hitler, July 19, 1940

## Section 1: Introduction

Germany surprised the world by defeating France in five-and-a-half weeks in May–June 1940. At the time, France was considered to be one of the strongest of the Allied nations.

On July 19, 1940, Adolf Hitler addressed the German Reichstag, which was sitting in the Berlin Kroll Opera House (where it had convened since the Communists burned the Reichstag building).

In this speech, Hitler dealt with the causes of the war, the campaigns of the previous ten months—including the invasion of Norway—and promoted a number of senior German army officers to high rank in reward for their efforts in the French campaign.

He then turned his speech toward the topic of peace. Saying that there was no sense in continuing the war, he offered an unconditional peace to Britain.

The peace offer was translated into English and printed by the tens of thousands on a four-page leaflet. These were then loaded into German aircraft, and dropped all over civilian areas in Britain, from Wales in the west, to Dover in the east.

This offer of peace was carried out even though the British Royal Air Force had been indiscriminately bombing German civilians since May 10, 1940, upon Churchill's direct orders.[1]

---

[1] In his speech, Hitler made reference to this systematic bombing campaign, and of the fact that German bombing to that time in the conflict had been limited to strategic military goals—and also warned that Germany would eventually retaliate—which it did in September 1940, in a campaign now often distorted to claim that the Germans started the "blitz."

As a result of the leafleting campaign, Hitler's peace offer became widely known among British civilians, to the point where considerable public opinion was aroused in its favor. This willingness to accept Hitler's offer was also represented at British Cabinet level, which was more or less evenly split on the matter.

Cabinet records released long after the war showed that those in favor of the peace offer included former Prime Minister Neville Chamberlain; Lord Halifax, the foreign minister; and Lord Beaverbrook, the press magnate. Halifax made the point in the cabinet discussion that Hitler's peace offer was "most reasonable."

Churchill, however, was having none of it, despite Halifax taking him outside in the garden of No. 10 Downing Street to try and personally persuade him.

Churchill then ordered an increase in the bombing campaign of civilian targets in Germany. In August 1940, as a direct answer to Hitler's peace offer, Churchill next ordered the first bombing of Berlin.

In doing this, the British leader knew full well that the Germans would be forced to respond—which they did the next month. The bombing of Berlin was Churchill's answer to Hitler's *Appeal for Peace and Sanity.*

## Section 2: Appeal for Peace and Sanity, July 19, 1940.

Deputies, Men of the German Reichstag!

In the midst of the mighty struggle for the freedom and future of the German nation, I have called on you to gather for this session today.

The grounds for it are: to give our people insight into the historic uniqueness of the events we have lived through; to express our thanks to the deserving soldiers; and to direct, once again and for the last time, an appeal to general reason.

Whoever contrasts the factors which triggered this historic conflict with the extent, the greatness, and consequence of the military occurrences, must realize that the events and sacrifices of this struggle stand in no relation to the alleged causes, unless

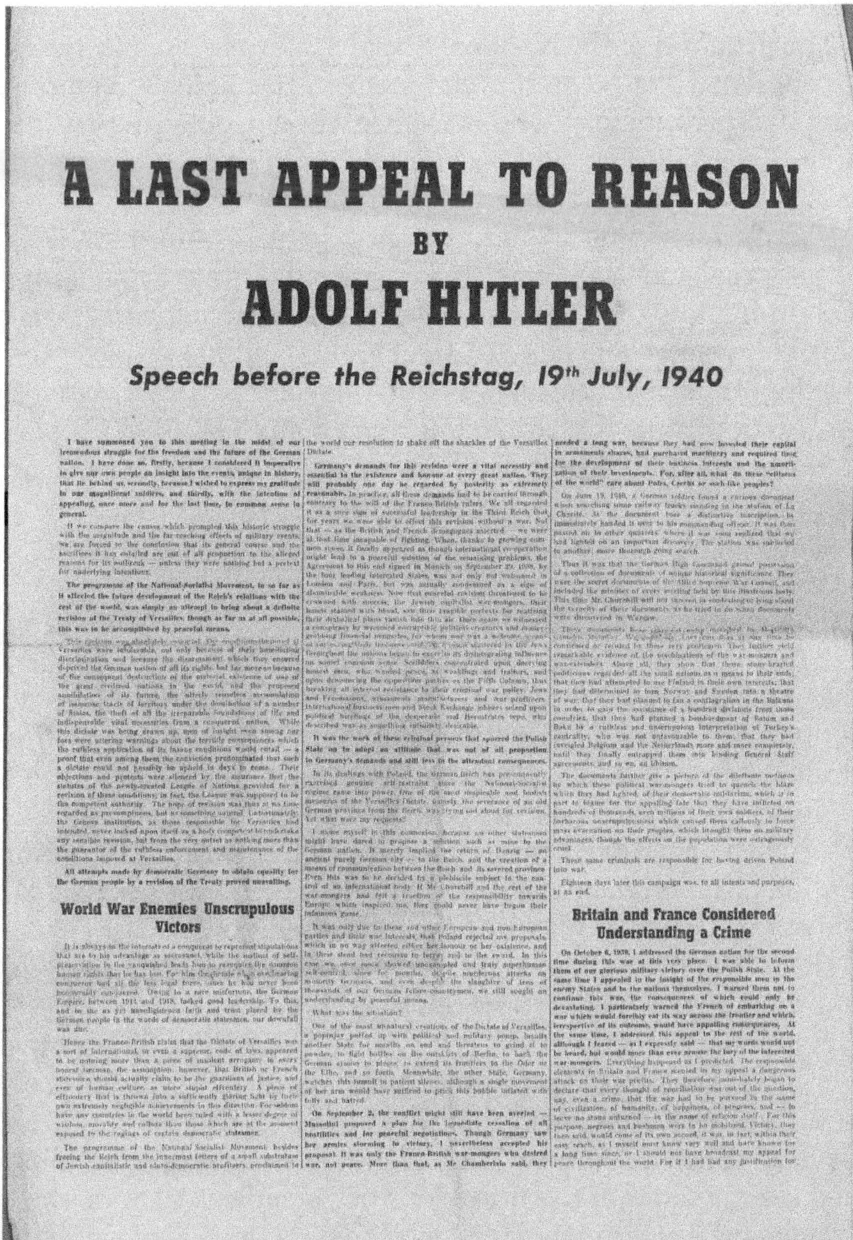

# A LAST APPEAL TO REASON

BY

# ADOLF HITLER

**Speech before the Reichstag, 19th July, 1940**

**I have summoned you to this meeting in the midst of our tremendous struggle for the freedom and the future of the German nation. I have done so, firstly, because I considered it imperative to give our own people an insight into the events, unique in history, that lie behind us, secondly, because I wished to express my gratitude to our magnificent soldiers, and thirdly, with the intention of appealing, once more and for the last time, to common sense in general.**

If we compare the causes which prompted this historic struggle with the magnitude and the far-reaching effects of military events, we are forced to the conclusion that its general course and the sacrifices it has entailed are out of all proportion to the alleged reasons for its outbreak — unless they were nothing but a pretext for underlying intentions.

**The programme of the National-Socialist Movement, in so far as it affected the future development of the Reich's relations with the rest of the world, was simply an attempt to bring about a definite revision of the Treaty of Versailles, though as far as at all possible, this was to be accomplished by peaceful means.**

## World War Enemies Unscrupulous Victors

## Britain and France Considered Understanding a Crime

***A copy of the "Appeal to Reason" leaflet dropped in the tens of thousands upon Britain by the Luftwaffe.***

these causes themselves were but pretexts for intentions yet concealed.

The program of the National Socialist Revolution, insofar as it concerned the future development of the Reich's relations with the surrounding world, was an attempt to obtain a revision of the Treaty of Versailles[2] under all circumstances-and as far as this was possible-by peaceful means.

This revision was by nature a necessity. The un-tenability of the provisions of Versailles lay not only in the humiliating discrimination, the disarmament of the German people secured with the result that they lost their rights, but above all in the resultant material destruction of the present and the intended destruction of the future of one of the greatest civilized peoples in the world, in the completely senseless accumulation of vast terrains under the mastery of a few states, in the depriving of the losers of irreplaceable foundations for life and indispensable vital goods.

The fact that insightful men on the side of the adversary, even while this *Diktat* was being composed, warned against the conclusive realization of the terms of this work of lunacy, is proof of the persuasion prevalent even in these ranks that it would be impossible to maintain this *Diktat* in the future.

Their misgivings and their protests were silenced by the assurance that the statutes of the newly created League of Nations secured the possibility of a revision of these provisions, indeed that it was authorized for such a revision.

At no time was hope for a revision regarded as something improper, but always as something quite natural.

Regrettably, contrary to the will of the men responsible for the Versailles *Diktat*, the institution in Geneva never regarded itself as an agency for procuring sensible revisions, but rather, from the beginning, as the custodian of the ruthless implementation and maintenance of the provisions of Versailles. All endeavors of democratic Germany failed to obtain, by means of revision,

---

[2] The treaty which ended the First World War. It blamed Germany for the war, stripped away 28,000 square miles of German land, and 6 million subjects. It also demanded impossible reparations from Germany, which smashed that country's economy.

an equality of rights for the German people. It lies in the interest of the victor to portray as universally sanctified those conditions that benefit him, while the essence of the instinct of self-preservation compels the vanquished to strive for a restoration of his general human rights.

For him this *Diktat*, penned by an arrogant enemy has even less force of law insofar as the victory of this enemy was a dishonest one. It was a rare misfortune that the German Reich was led exceedingly badly in the years 1914 to 1918!

To this, and to the not otherwise instructed trust and faith of the German people in the words of democratic statesmen, must our fall be ascribed.

It was thus that the joint British-French endeavor to portray the Versailles Treaty as some type of international or higher justice must have appeared to every honest German as nothing other than an insolent usurpation.

The supposition that British or French statesmen of all people were custodians of justice itself, or even of human culture, was a stupid effrontery. It was an affront which is sufficiently elucidated by their own inferior performances in these fields.

For rarely has this world been governed with a greater deficit of cleverness, morality, and culture than in that part of it which is presently at the mercy of the fury of certain democratic statesmen.

The National Socialist Movement has, besides its delivery from the Jewish-capitalist shackles imposed by a plutocratic-democratic, dwindling class of exploiters at home, pronounced its resolve to free the Reich from the shackles of the *Diktat* of Versailles abroad.

The German demands for a revision were an absolute necessity, a matter of course for the existence and the honor of any great people. Posterity will some day come to regard them as exceedingly modest.

All these demands had to be carried through, in practice against the will of the British-French potentates!

Now more than ever we all see it as a success of the leadership of the Third Reich that the realization of these revisions was possible for years without resort to war.

This was not the case-as the British and French demagogues would have it—because we were not then in a position to wage war.

When it finally appeared as though, thanks to a gradually awakening common sense, a peaceful resolution of the remaining problems could be reached through international cooperation, the agreement concluded in this spirit on September 29, 1938, at Munich by the four great states,[3] predominantly involved, was not welcomed by public opinion in London and Paris, but was condemned as a despicable sign of weakness.

The Jewish-capitalist warmongers, their hands covered with blood, saw in the possible success of such a peaceful revision the vanishing of plausible grounds for the realization of their insane plans. Once again that conspiracy of pitiful, corrupt political creatures and greedy financial magnates made its appearance, for whom war is a welcome means to bolster business.

The International Jewish poison of the peoples began to agitate against and to corrode healthy minds. Men of letters set out to portray decent men who desired peace as weaklings and traitors, to denounce opposition parties as a "fifth column," in order to eliminate internal resistance to their criminal policy of war.

Jews and Freemasons, armament industrialists and war profiteers, international traders and stock-traders, found political blackguards: desperados and glory seekers who represented war as something to be yearned for and hence wished for.

It is to be ascribed to these criminal elements that the Polish State was incited to assume a posture which stood in no relation

[3] The Munich Agreement of 1938 was an agreement signed by Germany, France, the United Kingdom, and Italy which allocated the German-majority regions of Sudetenland to the Reich, the Zaolzie area (with a Polish majority) to Poland, and the southern third of Slovakia and southern Carpathian Ruthenia to Hungary. The land allocations to Poland and Hungary are always ignored in the propaganda presentations of the Accord, which is always presented only as "Nazi aggression" instead of the peaceful restitution of territories illegally removed from three nations at the end of the First World War.

to the German demands and even less to the consequences that resulted.

The German Reich, in particular with regard to Poland, has shown restraint ever since the National Socialist rise to power.

One of the basest and stupidest provisions of the Versailles *Diktat*, namely the tearing away of an old German province from the Reich, already cried for a revision in and of itself.

But what was it that I demanded at the time?

I must in this context refer to my own person.

No other statesman could have afforded to propose a solution to the German nation in the way I did.

It comprised merely the return of Danzig—that is to say of an ancient, purely German city—to the Reich as well as the creation of a connection of the Reich to its severed province.

And this only pursuant to plebiscites conducted, in turn, under the auspices of an international forum.

If Mr. Churchill or any other warmongers had but a fraction of the sense of responsibility I felt toward Europe, they could not have played so perfidious a game.

***"Danzig greets its Führer!" reads this banner. Danzig, September 19, 1939***

For it need be ascribed solely to these vested interests in war, both within Europe and beyond, that Poland rejected the proposals which neither compromised its existence nor its honor, and instead resorted to terror and arms.

And it was truly superhuman restraint, without precedent, which for months led us, in spite of persistent assassination attempts on ethnic Germans-yes, indeed, in spite of the slaughter of tens of thousands of German nationals, to continue to search for a path toward peaceful understanding.

For what was the situation like?

One of the creations of the *Diktat* of Versailles, the most divorced from reality, a bogey,[4] inflated militarily and politically, insulted a state[5] for many months, threatening to beat it, to fight battles before Berlin, to smash the German Army to pieces, to transfer the border to the Oder or the Elbe; it went on and on.

And this other state, Germany, watched the goings-on patiently for months, although one good swipe would have sufficed for us to burst this bubble, that was inflated by stupidity and arrogance!

On September 2, this struggle could yet have been avoided. Mussolini made a proposal to put an immediate end to the hostilities and to negotiate peacefully.

Though Germany saw its armies advancing victoriously, I accepted this nonetheless.

But the Anglo-French warmongers needed war, not peace.

And they needed a long war, as Mr. Chamberlain[6] put the matter at the time. It was to last for at least three years, since they had in the meantime invested their capital in the armament industry, bought the necessary machinery, and now needed the precondition of time for the thriving of their business and for the amortization of their investments.

And besides: what are Poles, Czechs, or other such nationalities to these citizens of the world?

A German soldier found a curious document while rummaging through train wagons at the La Charite station on June 19,

---

[4] Poland.

[5] Germany.

[6] Neville Chamberlain, Prime Minister of Britain until May 10, 1940.

1940. He immediately handed over the document—which bore a particular remark—to his superiors at departmental headquarters. From there the paper passed to agencies. It became clear that what had been discovered constituted evidence in a most important investigation.

The train station was once more thoroughly searched. And it was thus that the High Command of the Wehrmacht came into possession of a collection of documents of unique historical significance.

What was found were the secret files of the Allied High War Council, including the protocols of all sessions of this illustrious association.

And this time it shall not be possible for Mr. Churchill to simply deny or to lie about the authenticity of these documents, as he had attempted to do at the time in the case of documents found in Warsaw.[7]

For these documents feature handwritten notes in the margins penned by Gamelin, Daladier, Weygand, and so on. Hence these gentlemen are free either to admit to these or to disown them at any time.

And these documents enlighten us as to the dealings of these gentlemen who have an interest in the war and in its expansion.

They will above all demonstrate how these cold-blooded politicians and military men have used all these small peoples as a means to an end; how they tried to subject Finland to their interests; how they determined to make Norway and Sweden the theater of war; how they planned to set fire to the Balkans to procure the assistance of 100 divisions from there; how they prepared to bomb Batum and Baku under the cover of a shrewd as well as unscrupulous reading of the Turkish neutrality in favor of their own interests; how they spun their web around the Netherlands and Belgium, pulling its strings constantly tighter, and finally engaging them in general staff agreements; as well as many other things.

The documents afford us, moreover, a good picture of the entire amateurish method which these policy-making warmongers employed in an attempt to contain the fire they had

[7] Published in the *German White Book* on the Polish crisis.

kindled. These speak of their military pseudo-democracy which is jointly responsible for the gruesome fate which they have inflicted on hundreds of thousands and millions of soldiers of their own countries; of their barbaric lack of conscience which led them to drive their own peoples from their homes in cold blood and deliberately, in a mass evacuation whose military consequences were not necessarily favorable to them, while the general human results were shockingly gruesome.

The same criminals are at the same time responsible for whipping up the Poles and inciting them to war. Eighteen days later this campaign ended-for all practical purposes.

For a second time in the war, I spoke to the German people from this stand on October 6, 1939.

I was then able to report to it the glorious military defeat of the Polish State.

I then also directed an appeal to reason to the men responsible in the enemy states and to their peoples. I warned against further pursuit of the war, the consequences of which could only be devastating.

I warned the French especially not to start a war which, by necessity, would eat its way inward from the frontier and which, irrespective of its outcome, would have dire consequences.

At this time, I directed an appeal to the rest of the world as well. However, as I said then, I did so with the apprehension that not only might I not be heard, but that thereby I might only elicit the wrath of the warmongers interested. And this is precisely what came to pass. The responsible elements in England and France smelt a rat, seeing my appeal as a dangerous assault on their lucrative profiteering in the war.

Thus they hurriedly and eagerly declared that any thought of an understanding was a waste of time—yes, that this would even have to be regarded as a crime. The war had to be pursued in the name of culture, humanity, good fortune, progress, civilization, and—Good God! —even in the name of sacred religion, and in subservience to this end, even Negroes and bushmen[8] had to be mobilized.

[8] *Buschmenschen* in the original German. Refers to native nonwhite soldiers from the French and British colonies.

***German troops light a cigarette for an African soldier serving with the French army, captured during the Battle for France, 1940.***

And then, of course, victory would come about of its own accord, so to speak. It would then be within grasp; one need only reach out for it, so they said. I was very well aware of all this myself, and indeed had known it for a long time, and it was only because of this, that I had laid before the world my appeal for peace.

For, if I were in a position to believe in victory, I would not have approached England and France with an understanding without any conditions attached.

In a few days these agitators succeeded in portraying me as a coward before the eyes of the world.

I was scolded for my peace proposal, even personally insulted. Mr. Chamberlain[9] virtually spat in my face before the world public and declined to even talk of peace, according to the directives of the warmongers and agitators backing him: Churchill, Duff Cooper,[10] Eden,[11] Hore-Belisha,[12] and so on. Not to mention negotiating a peace.

And it was thus that the big capitalist clique of war profiteers cried for a continuation of the war. And this continuation has now begun.

I have already asserted, and all of you, my fellow citizens, I know this: that if I do not speak for some time, or nothing much happens, then this does not mean that I am doing nothing. With us it is not necessary to multiply by a factor of five or twelve every airplane built, and then to proclaim it loudly to the world.

Besides, hens would be ill-advised to cry out to the world every egg just laid. It would be all the more ill-considered of

[9] Neville Chamberlain, Prime Minister of Britain.

[10] Alfred Duff Cooper, British Cabinet War Secretary in 1935, promoted to First Lord of the Admiralty in 1937, and Minister of Information under the Winston Churchill prime ministership in 1940. A notorious warmonger in British politics.

[11] Robert Anthony Eden, British Foreign Secretary who resigned from the Chamberlain cabinet in 1938 in opposition to the attempts by the latter to avoid war. Appointed by Churchill in May 1940 as Cabinet Secretary of State for War.

[12] Leslie Hore-Belisha, a British Jew appointed by Neville Chamberlain as Secretary of State for War. He held the office until May 1940,.

statesmen to announce projects barely beyond the planning stage, in nervous chatter, to the surrounding world, so as to inform it in a timely manner.

To the excited garrulousness of two of these great democratic state leaders[13] we owe ever-current information on the plans for an expansion of the war by our adversaries, and especially on the concentration of the war effort in Norway and Sweden.

While the Anglo-French clique of warmongers was on the lookout for new opportunities to expand the war, and trying to trap new victims, I have labored to bring to a conclusion the organizational buildup of the Wehrmacht, to set up new units, to start up production for the war, to get material to flow, as well as to order training of the entire Wehrmacht for its new missions.

Beyond this, however, the bad weather of the late autumn and winter forced a postponement of military operations.

In the course of the month of March, we gained knowledge of British-French ambitions to intervene in the Russo-Finnish conflict;[14] which was less to help the Finns and more to damage Russia, the latter being seen as a power cooperating with Germany.

This ambition grew into the determination to intervene actively in Finland itself and, if possible, to gain a base for carrying the war to the Baltic Sea.

And, at this time also, suggestions of the Allied High War Council appeared with ever greater insistence either to set afire the Balkans or Asia Minor in an effort to bar the Reich from its Russian and Romanian oil imports, or to gain possession of

[13] Britain and France.

[14] The Winter War was a military conflict between the Soviet Union and Finland in 1939–1940. It began with the Soviet invasion of Finland on November 30, 1939 (three months after the outbreak of World War II), and ended with the Moscow Peace Treaty on March 13, 1940. The League of Nations deemed the attack illegal and expelled the Soviet Union from the League on December 14, 1939. The British and French governments somehow "overlooked" this aggression by the Soviet Union—as they did the Soviet invasion of Poland on September 17, 1939—and made no declaration of war as they had done against Germany.

Swedish iron ore. Landings in Norway were to serve this end with the goal of occupying all ore railroads leading from Narvik across Sweden to the port of Lulea.

The Russo-Finnish peace accords prevented, at the last minute, the carrying out of the already envisioned action in the Nordic States.

Yet, merely a few days later, similar ambitions surfaced anew and precipitated a clear decision.

England and France had agreed to move, in one sudden strike, to occupy numerous important locations in Norway under the pretext of preventing further support for the German war effort with Swedish ore.

To secure access completely to the Swedish ore, they intended to march into Sweden themselves and to push aside the few forces Sweden could muster, either, if possible, in a friendly manner or, if necessary, by force.

Of the imminence of this danger we were informed personally by the untameable garrulousness of the First Lord of the British Admiralty.

Moreover, we received confirmation through a hint made by the French Premier Reynaud[15] in a talk with a foreign diplomat. That the date had been postponed twice before the eighth of April, and that the occupation was scheduled for the eighth, that the eighth, therefore, was the third and final day—of this we gained knowledge only recently.

It was conclusively established only with the discovery of the protocols of the High Allied War Council. I then ordered the Wehrmacht, as soon as the danger of dragging the North into the war was becoming apparent, to take the appropriate measures.

The case of the *Altmark*[16] already demonstrated that the Norwegian Government was not willing to uphold its neutrality. Beyond this, reports of secret agents also revealed that, at least

---

[15] Paul Reynaud, Prime Minister of the Third Republic, noted for his militant opposition to Germany.

[16] A German ship illegally boarded and seized in February 1940 by the Royal Navy upon Churchill's direct orders, in then neutral Norway's waters in contravention of international neutrality conventions.

***A British aerial reconnaissance photograph of the* Altmark *in Norway's Jøssingfjord.***

***German dead from the* Altmark *are brought ashore for burial after the incident.***

insofar as the leading heads of the Norwegian Government and the Allies were concerned, there was already full agreement.

Finally, Norway's reaction to the violation of its territory by British minelayers dispelled all remaining doubts.

The German operation, prepared down to the last detail, was launched. In fact the situation was a bit different from what we perceived it to be on April 9.

While we then believed, we had anticipated the British occupation by a few hours, we know today that the landing of the English troops had been scheduled for the eighth.

The deployment of the British contingents had already begun on the fifth and sixth. However, the moment the first news reached the British Admiralty of the German steps, i.e. that a German fleet had put to sea, this development so impressed Mr. Churchill that he decided to have the contingents already embarked disembark once again, so that the British fleet would first be able to search for and attack German ships. This attempt ended in failure.

Only a single English destroyer came into contact with the German naval forces and was shot out of the water.

This vessel could not relay any sort of message to the British Admiralty or to the fleet of the English naval combat contingents.

And thus, on the ninth, the landing of German forward units was carried out along a coastal front stretching from Oslo north to Narvik. When news of this reached London, the First Lord of the Admiralty, Mr. Churchill, had already been on the lookout for many hours-eagerly awaiting first reports of the successes of his fleet.

And this strike, my Deputies, was the most daring undertaking in the history of German warfare!

Its successful implementation was possible only thanks to the leadership and the behavior of all German soldiers involved.

What our three arms, the Army, the Navy, and the Luftwaffe, have accomplished in the struggle for Norway assures them mention in the records of the highest soldiership.

The Navy conducted its operations, and later handled the troop transports, faced by an enemy who, all in all, possessed an almost tenfold superiority. All units of our young Reich War Navy have covered themselves with eternal glory in this venture. Only after the war will it be appropriate to discuss the difficulties faced especially in this campaign: the numerous unexpected setbacks, losses, and accidents suffered.

To have overcome all this in the end goes to the credit of the behavior, the leadership, and the troops.

The Luftwaffe, which often was the only means of transport and communications in so gigantically vast a terrain, outdid itself in all respects.

Death-defying attacks on the enemy, on his ships and landing troops, are hardly more impressive than the tenacious heroics of the transport plane pilots, who in spite of unimaginably adverse weather started time and time again on their way to the land of the midnight sun, only to unload soldiers or freight in the midst of a snow storm. Norway's fjords have become the graveyard of many a British warship.

Because of the uninterrupted wild attacks of German bombers and Stukas, the British fleet was forced to retreat from and to evacuate the very arena of which a few weeks earlier an English newspaper had so tastefully stated "that it would be a pleasure for England to oblige the German invitation to do battle there."

The crossing already constituted a great challenge for the soldiers of the Army.

In a few cases, airborne troops had opened up the area where they first set foot. Then division after division flooded the land which, due to its natural characteristics, already possessed considerable defenses, and which—as far as the Norwegian units were concerned—was very valiantly defended.

Of the Englishmen who had landed in Norway, one can say that the only remarkable thing was the unscrupulousness with which such badly trained, insufficiently equipped, and miserably led soldiers had been put ashore as an expeditionary corps.

From the beginning, they were certain to lose. By contrast, what our German infantry, the pioneers, what our artillery, our communications and construction units, have achieved in Norway can only be termed the proud heroism of struggle and labor. The word Narvik will enter our history as glorious evidence of the spirit of the Wehrmacht of the National Socialist Greater German Reich.

The gentlemen Churchill, Chamberlain, Daladier,[17] and so on, have, until recently, been exceedingly ill-informed as to the essence of the Greater German unification process.

At the time, I announced that the future would probably teach them better. And I may well assume that in particular the deployment of mountain troops from the Ostmark[18] at this front furthest north in our battle for freedom has enlightened them sufficiently as far as the Greater German Reich and its sons are concerned.

It is lamentable that the grenadiers of Mr. Chamberlain did not pay sufficient and, above all, persistent attention to this conflict, and instead preferred to be satisfied with the first test of the inner disposition of the tribes of our nation which have newly come to the Reich.

General von Falkenhorst led operations in Norway. Lieutenant General Dietl was the hero of Narvik.

Operations at sea were conducted under the leadership of Admiral General Saalwachter and the Admirals Carls and Boehm, and Vice Admiral Lutjens.

Operations of the Luftwaffe were under the leadership of Colonel General Milch and Lieutenant General Geissler.

The High Command of the Wehrmacht, Colonel General Keitel, as the Chief of the High Command, and General Jodl, as the Chief of the Wehrmacht leadership staff, were responsible for implementing my directives for the entire undertaking.

Even before the conclusion of the campaign in Norway, news in the West took on an ever more threatening character.

While, in fact, preparations had been made before the war to break through the Maginot Line in the event of a necessary conflict with France or England, an undertaking for which the German troops had been trained and had been equipped

---

[17] Édouard Daladier, radical politician and three-time Prime Minister of France. He publicly rejected Hitler's peace proposal of October 6, 1939, against the wishes of many in the French government.
[18] Austria.

with the weaponry required, the course of events in the first months of the war compelled us to contemplate the possibility of moving against Holland and Belgium.

While Germany had positioned hardly any units against Belgium or the Netherlands, other than those necessary for security reasons, as well as beginning to expand upon its fortification system, a visible mass of French units began to array itself along the French-Belgian border.

In particular, the concentration of tanks and motorized divisions in this sector revealed that it was intended—at any rate it was possible—for these to be hurled at lighting speed through Belgium at the German border.

Decisive in this context was the following observation: While, in the case of a loyal reading of the Belgian-Dutch neutrality, these two countries would have been forced, by the concentration of strong Anglo-French forces at their border, to focus their attention on the West, both began to reduce their troop strengths along this border to the same degree they began to build up the units stationed along the border with Germany.

News of ongoing talks at the general staff-level, also shed a peculiar light on Belgian-Dutch neutrality. I need not emphasize

***German tanks sweep through France, May 1940.***

that these talks, had they been conducted in the spirit of true neutrality, would have had to be held with both sides.

Besides this, such an intensification of signs indicating that a move of the Anglo-French troops across Holland and Belgium against the German industrial area was taking place required that we should regard this threat as a serious danger.

Hence I took the German Wehrmacht into my confidence, informing it of the possibility of such a development and entrusting it with the appropriate, detailed directives.

In numerous conferences at the High Command of the Wehrmacht with the Commanders in Chief of the three branches of the Wehrmacht, the leaders of the Army groups and of the armies, down to the leaders of important, individual undertakings, the tasks facing us were enumerated and thoroughly discussed. Among the troops these were taken up with great understanding, as the basis for a special type of training.

Correspondingly, the entire German deployment underwent the necessary adjustments.

The thorough observations which had been conducted everywhere gradually led to the compelling recognition that, from the beginning of May on, an Anglo-French advance had to be expected at any moment.

In the days of May 6 and 7, telephone conversations between London and Paris took place, of which we gained intelligence and which reinforced suspicions that an invasion of the Netherlands and Belgium by the so-called Allies had to be expected at any moment.

Thus on the following day, May 8, I ordered an immediate attack for May 10, at 5:35 in the morning.

The basic thought behind this operation was to deploy, without worrying about peripheral successes, the entire Wehrmacht—especially the Army and the Luftwaffe—in so decisive a manner, that the envisioned operations had to attain the complete annihilation of the Anglo-French forces.

In contrast to the Schlieffen Plan[19] of the year 1914, I ordered

[19] The Schlieffen Plan was a 1905 plan drawn up in the event of an outbreak of war against Germany on two fronts. It foresaw an attack

the main thrust of the operation along the left flank of the breakthrough front, while, however, keeping up appearances of a reversed version.

This deception was successful. Conduct of the entire operation was made easy for me by measures our adversaries themselves took. For the concentration of the entire Anglo-French motorized combat forces against Belgium revealed as certain that the High Command of the Allied armies had arrived at the decision to advance most speedily into this area.

We relied on the steadfastness of all German infantry divisions deployed in the thrust against the right flank of the Anglo-French motorized Army Group. Such a drive had to lead to its complete shattering and dissolution—yes, perhaps even to its encirclement.

As a second operation, I had planned the taking of the Seine up to Le Havre, as well as securing bases at the Somme and Aisne for a third assault.

This was intended to break through, with strong forces across the plateau at Langres, to the Swiss border. Reaching the coast south of Bordeaux was to conclude operations. Within this framework and in this sequence, operations were in fact carried out.

The success of this mightiest sequence of battles in world history we owe first and foremost to the German soldier himself. He held his own at all places he was deployed to the highest degree. The German tribes all share equally in this glory.

The soldiers of the young, new *Reichsgaus*,[20] added only since 1938, also fought in an exemplary fashion and took a heavy toll of lives. The heroic risk of life by all Germans in this war will make the emerging National Socialist Greater German Reich

---

on France via Belgium and required six weeks to defeat the French, before the bulk of the German army could turn east to ward off a Russian attack. The plan nearly succeeded in August 1914, but was thrown off track by the first Battle of the Marne and the introduction of the stalemate trench warfare of the First World War.

[20] A *gau* was an administrative area in the Reich, akin to a province, a state, or a county. The new *Reichsgaus* referred to here are those of Austria.

eternally sacred and dear not only to the present generation, but to all that follow.

When I undertake to honor all those forces to whose activities we owe this most glorious of victories, then first mention is due to a leadership which, in particular in this campaign, has met the highest of requirements.

The Army:

It has performed the tasks imposed upon it, under the leadership of Colonel General von Brauchitsch and his Chief of Staff Halder, in a truly glorious fashion.

If the leadership of the German Army of long ago was regarded as the best in the world, then it is deserving today of at least equal admiration. Yes, since success is decisive for passing judgment, the leadership of the new German Army must be considered even better!

Subdivided into three Army Groups, the Army in the West was placed under the orders of Colonel Generals Ritter von Leeb, von Rundstedt, and von Bock.

The Army Group of General Ritter von Leeb had the initial mission to maintain the left flank of the German front in the West, stretching from the Swiss border up to the Moselle, in a state of highest defensive readiness. It was anticipated that, in the later course of the operation, this front would also actively intervene in the battle of destruction with two armies under the leadership of Colonel General von Witzleben and General Dollmann.

At 5:35 in the morning of May 10, the two Army Groups under Colonel Generals von Rundstedt and von Bock launched the attack.

It was their mission, along the entire front from the river Moselle to the North Sea, to break through the enemy lines along the frontier; to occupy the Netherlands; to move against Antwerp and the troops stationed at Dyle; to take Liege; and, above all, to reach the left flank along the river Meuse with massive forces for the attack, to force a crossing between Namur and Carignan with a main thrust of the tank and motorized divisions at Sedan and, in the further course of operations, to assemble all available tank and motorized divisions to push onward, along the system of canals and rivers between the Aisne and the Somme, to the sea.

To Rundstedt's southern Army Group fell also the important task of preventing a repetition of the Miracle of the Marne of 1914. He was to accomplish this task by securing, according to plan, the cover of the left flank in the course of the breakthrough.

This massive operation, which already decided the further course of the war, led, as planned, to the annihilation of the main mass of the French Army as well as of the entire British Expeditionary Force, and already added luster to the German leadership.

Besides the two leaders of the Army Groups and their Chiefs of Staff, Lieutenant General von Sodenstern and Lieutenant General von Salmuth, the following leaders of the Army are deserving of the highest of distinctions:

Colonel General von Kluge as leader of the Fourth Army;
Colonel General List as leader of the Twelfth Army;
Colonel General von Reichenau as leader of the Sixth Army;
General von Kuchler as leader of the Eighteenth Army;

***French prisoners-of-war, June 1940. Most were disarmed and sent home by the Germans after France surrendered.***

General Busch as leader of the Sixteenth Army; and the Generals von Kleist, Guderian, Hoth, and Hoeppner as leaders of the tank and motorized troops.

Large additional numbers of generals and officers who distinguished themselves in these operations are known to you already, my Deputies, because of the high distinctions granted them.

The further conduct of the operation in the general direction of the Aisne and the Seine was not intended to conquer Paris primarily, but rather to create, or better secure, a basis for a breakthrough to the Swiss border. This massive offensive action, thanks to the outstanding leadership of all grades, also went according to plan.

A change of personnel in the High Command of the French Army, which had meanwhile taken place, was to revive its resistance and to bring about a change, much desired by the Allies, in the fortunes of the battle so unhappily begun.

Indeed it was possible to get the German armies and their offensive actions going at several locations only after

***French President Marshal Pétain meets Adolf Hitler at Montoire. Foreign Minister Joachim von Ribbentrop at the right, October 24, 1940.***

overcoming the strongest of resistance. Here, not only the courage, but also the training of the German soldier had the opportunity to hold its own to a high degree. Inspired by the zeal of countless officers and noncommissioned officers, as well as of individual men of valor, the infantry itself, time and time again, was compelled onward even in the most difficult of situations.

Paris fell! The breaking of the enemy's resistance at the Aisne opened the way to a breakthrough to the Swiss border.

In one gigantic envelopment the armies stormed to the back of the Maginot Line. Now abandoning its reserve, the Army Group Leeb went on the offensive in two locations west of Saarbrucken and Neubreisach.

Under orders from Generals von Witzleben and Dollmann, they achieved the breakthrough. And thus it was possible not only to surround the gigantic front of the French resistance, but to dissolve it into little particles and to force it to the well-known capitulation.

These operations were crowned by the now generally beginning advance of the German armies. At their head moved the incomparable Panzer and motor divisions of the Army with the goal of driving a left flank down the Rhone in the direction of Marseilles, and a right flank across the Loire in the direction of Bordeaux and the Spanish border.

This was to destroy the dissolving remains of the French Army, or rather to occupy French territory. I will report in detail at a later point on the intervention of our allies in this war. When Marshal Pétain [21] offered France's laying down of arms,[22] he was not laying down a weapon he still held. Rather

---

[21] Henri Philippe Benoni Omer Joseph Pétain, French general appointed Premier of France by President Lebrun in June 1940. Faced with defeat on all fronts, the French cabinet resolved to make peace with Germany. The French government retained nominal control over the northern half of France, and full sovereignty over the southern half. Because the government was based at the southern French city of Vichy at the time of the surrender, the Pétain-ruled state became known as Vichy France.

[22] June 22, 1940.

he merely put an end to a situation completely untenable in the eyes of every soldier.

Only the bloody dilettantism of a Mr. Churchill either fails to comprehend as much or lies about it in spite of better knowledge.

In the second, third, and last phase of this war, the following Army leaders distinguished themselves as did the earlier mentioned generals:

Colonel General von Witzleben; the Generals von Weichs, Dollmann, Strauss. The valiant divisions and standards of the Waffen SS also fought within the framework of these armies.

When I express my gratitude and that of the German people to the aforementioned generals, in their capacity as leaders of the Army and Army Groups, this applies at the same time to all other officers, all of whom it is not possible to mention by name, and especially to all the nameless workers of the General Staff. In this battle, my Deputies, the rank and file of Germany has proved itself to be what it has always been: the best infantry in the world!

And with it all other branches of the Army compete: artillery and pioneers, and, above all, the young units of our tanks and motorized troops.

The German Panzer weapon, through this war, has made its entry into world history. The men of the Waffen SS share in the glory.

Yet the communications units, the construction units of the pioneers, the railroad construction men, etc., are also worthy, in accordance with their performance, of the highest praise we have to offer.

In the wake of the armies followed the commandos of the Todt Organization,[23] of the Reich Labor Service,[24] and of the

---

[23] The *Organisation Todt* was a Third Reich civil and military engineering group in Germany named after its founder, Fritz Todt, an engineer and senior Nazi figure. The organization was responsible for a huge range of engineering projects both in pre-World War II Germany, in Germany itself, and occupied territories from France to the Soviet Union during the war.

[24] The *Reichsarbeitsdienst:* the Reich Labor Service, originally

NSKK,[25] and these also helped to repair roads, bridges, as well as to restore order to traffic.

Within the framework of the Army, this time there also fought parts of the Flak artillery of our Luftwaffe. At the foremost front, they helped to break the enemy's power of resistance and attack. A detailed account of their effectiveness can be rendered only at a later date.

The Luftwaffe itself:

At dawn on the morning of May 10, thousands of fighter planes and dive bombers, under the cover of fighters and destroyers, descended on enemy airfields.

Within a few days uncontested air superiority was assured. And not for one minute in the further course of the battle was it allowed to slip.

Only where temporarily no German airplanes were sighted, could enemy fighters and bombers make short appearances. Besides this, their activities were restricted to night action.

The Field Marshal[26] had the Luftwaffe under his orders during this mission in the war.

Its tasks were:

1. To destroy the enemy air forces, i.e. to remove these from the skies;

2. To support directly or indirectly the fighting troops by uninterrupted attacks;

3. To destroy the enemy's means of command and movement;

4. To wear down and break the enemy's morale and will to resist;

---

organized to alleviate the mass unemployment which plagued Germany prior to 1933. From June 1935 onward, men aged between 18 and 24 had to serve six months before their military service.

[25] *Nationalsozialistisches Kraftfahrkorps:* The National Socialist Motor Corps. Originally part of the S.A. (*Sturmabteilung*, or Brownshirts), this party organization specialized in training party members in the driving and handling of motor vehicles. After 1933, it was absorbed into the state and became a roadside assistance group, comparable to the present-day Automobile Association. From 1935 onward, the NSKK also provided training for Panzer crews of the German Army.

[26] Hermann Göring.

5. To land parachute troops as advance units.

The manner of their deployment in the operation in general, as well as their adjustment to the tactical demands of the moment, was exceptional. Without the valor of the Army, the successes attained should never have been possible.

Equally true is it that, without the heroic mission of the Luftwaffe, the valor of the Army should have been for naught. Both Army and Luftwaffe are deserving of the greatest glory! The deployment of the Luftwaffe in the West took place under the personal command of Field Marshal Göring. His Chief of Staff: Major General Jeschonnek.

Both aerial fleets stood under orders of General der Flieger Sperrle and General der Flieger Kesselring.

The Aviation Corps subordinate to them stood under orders of Generals der Flieger Grauert and Keller, Lieutenant General Loerzer, and Lieutenant General Ritter von Greim, as well as of Major General Freiherr von Richthofen.

Both Flak Corps stood under orders of Flak Artillery General Weise and Major General Dessloch.

The Ninth Aerial Division under Major General Coeler deserves special mention.

The Commander of the Parachute Troops, General der Flieger Student, was severely wounded. The further conduct of

***A platoon from the* Reicharbietsdiesnt, *1940.***

the battle in the air in Norway was orchestrated by General der Flieger Stumpff.

While millions of German soldiers of the Army, Luftwaffe, and Waffen SS took part in these battles, others could not be spared at home as they were needed for the buildup of the local reserve formations.

Many of the most capable officers—as bitter as this was for them—were forced to conduct and oversee the training of those soldiers who, as reserve units, or perhaps in new formations, were to go to the front only later.

Despite my sympathy for the inner sentiments of those who felt at a disadvantage, the greater common interest, as a matter of principle, was decisive.

Party and State, Army, Navy, Luftwaffe, and SS sent every man to the front whom they were able to spare somehow.

Yet, without securing a Replacement Army, a reserve air force, reserve SS formations, as well as Party and State in general, the war at the front could not have been waged.

As the organizers of the Replacement Army at home and of the armament and supplies for the Luftwaffe, the following have attained special merit: Artillery General Fromm and General der Flieger Udet.

I cannot conclude the enumeration of all these meritorious generals and admirals without paying tribute to those who are my closest co-workers in the Staff of the High Command of the Wehrmacht:

Colonel General Keitel as Chief of the High Command of the Wehrmacht, and Major General Jodl as his Chief of Staff. They have made the greatest of contributions to the realization of my plans and ideas throughout long months of many cares and much work.

An appreciation of the accomplishments of our Navy and its leaders will only be possible, to a full extent, at the end of the war.

When I now conclude these purely military reflections on events, truth compels me to state the historic fact that none of this would have been possible without the disposition of the home front-or without, at its fore, the foundation, the work, and the activities of the National Socialist Party. Already in 1919, in the age of great decline, it proclaimed its program for the establishment of a German People's Army and has stood up for it throughout the decades with a zealous determination.

Without its activities, the conditions necessary for both the re-emergence of the German Reich and the creation of a German Wehrmacht would not have existed.

Above all, it lent the struggle its ideological world view. To the senseless sacrifice of life of our democratic opponents in the interests of their plutocracies, it opposes the defense of a national interest. Its activities have resulted in a solidarity between front and homeland, which regrettably did not exist in the World War. From its ranks, therefore, I should like to name the men, who along with countless others, attained great merit in securing the opportunity to celebrate victory in a new Germany: Party comrade Reich Minister Hess,[27] himself an old soldier of the World War, has been one of the most loyal fighters for the erection of the present state and its Wehrmacht ever since the early days of the foundation of the Movement.

Party comrade Chief of Staff of the SA Lutze has organized the mass of millions of SA men, in the sense of supporting the state to the utmost, and has secured its pre- and post-military training.

Party comrade Himmler has organized the entire security of our Reich as well as the units of the Waffen SS.

Party comrade Hierl has been the founder and leader of the Reich Labor Service.

Party comrade Ley is the guarantor of the behavior of the German worker.

Party comrade and Reich Minister Major General Todt is the organizer of the production of armament and ammunition and has gained eternal merit as a master builder in the construction of our massive, strategic road network as well as of the fortified front in the West.

Party comrade Minister Goebbels is the leader of a propaganda apparatus whose refinement is best ascertained in comparison with that of the World War.

---

[27] Rudolf Hess, Hitler's deputy leader until 1941.

Among the numerous organizations of the home front, there remain to be mentioned the organization of the *Kriegswinterhilfswerk,*[28] and of the *Nationalsozialistische Volkswohlfahrt*[29] under the leadership of Party comrade Hilgenfeldt, as well as the German Red Cross, and moreover the *Reichsluftschutzbund*[30] under the leadership of Flak Artillery General von Schroeder.

I cannot conclude this tribute without thanking the one man who, for years, has engaged himself in loyal, untiring, self-devouring work to realize my foreign policy directives.

The name of Party comrade von Ribbentrop[31] as Reich Foreign Minister shall remain tied for all eternity to the political rise of the German nation.

My Deputies!

I have determined, as Führer and Supreme Commander of the German Wehrmacht, to honor the most meritorious generals before the one forum which in truth represents the entire German nation.

I must place at their forefront a man to whom I have difficulty in expressing sufficient gratitude for the services which tie his

---

[28] The "War Winter Relief" (literally "winter help work") was an annual drive by the *Nationalsozialistische Volkswohlfahrt* (the National Socialist People's Welfare Organization), to help finance charitable work. Its slogan was "None shall starve nor freeze." It ran from 1933–1945 during the months of October through March, and was designed to provide food, clothing, coal, and other items to less fortunate Germans during the inclement months. Similar initiatives were started in countries in German-occupied Europe.

[29] See note 27 above.

[30] The State Air Protection Corps, founded in 1933 as a branch of the German Aviation Ministry. The group's first function was to serve as Air Defense crews during a period when Germany was forbidden an air force by the Treaty of Versailles. In 1935, the *Reichsluftschutzbund* was placed under the authority of the Luftwaffe and performed mainly non-combat support roles such as ground crew training and search and rescue. During World War II, the *Reichsluftschutzbund* performed in air defense support manning anti-aircraft emplacements in Germany's major cities.

[31] Joachim von Ribbentrop, foreign minister.

name to the Movement, to the State, and, above all, to the German Luftwaffe.

Since the days of the foundation of the SA, Party Comrade Göring has been bound up in the development and rise of the Movement. Since we came to power, his capacity for work and willingness to take responsibility have accomplished deeds in numerous fields for the German nation and the German Reich which cannot be excluded from the history of our nation and Reich.

Since the rebuilding of the German Wehrmacht, he has become the creator of the German Luftwaffe. It is granted to only a few mortals to create in the course of their lives a military instrument practically from nothing and to transform it into the mightiest weapon of its kind in the world. Above all, he has lent it his spirit.

Field Marshal Göring as creator of the German Luftwaffe, and as an individual man, has made the greatest contribution to

***Hermann Göring as president of the Reichstag.***

the rebuilding of the German Wehrmacht. As the leader of the German Luftwaffe he has, in the course of the war up to date, created the prerequisites for victory. His merits are unequalled! I name him Reichsmarschall of the Greater German Reich and award him the Grand Cross of the Iron Cross.

For services rendered to the victory of German weaponry in the struggle for the freedom and future of our Greater German Reich, I hereby promote:

The Commander in Chief of the Army, Colonel General von Brauchitsch, to the rank of Field Marshal;

Colonel General von Rundstedt, Commander in Chief of Army Group A, to the rank of Field Marshal;

Colonel General Ritter von Leeb, Commander in Chief of Army Group C, to the rank of Field Marshal;

Colonel General von Bock, Commander in Chief of Army Group B, to the rank of Field Marshal;

Colonel General List, Commander in Chief of the Twelfth Army, to the rank of Field Marshal;

Colonel General von Kluge, Commander in Chief of the Fourth Army, to the rank of Field Marshal;

Colonel General von Witzleben, Commander in Chief of the First Army, to the rank of Field Marshal;

Colonel General von Reichenau, Commander in Chief of the Sixth Army, to the rank of Field Marshal.

I promote:

General Dollmann, Commander in Chief of the Seventh Army, to the rank of Colonel General;

General Freiherr von Weichs, Commander in Chief of the Second Army, to the rank of Colonel General;

General von Kuchler, Commander in Chief of the Eighteenth Army, to the rank of Colonel General;

General Busch, Commander in Chief of the Sixteenth Army, to the rank of Colonel General; General Strauss, Commander in Chief of the Ninth Army, to the rank of Colonel General; General von Falkenhorst, Military Commander in Norway, to the rank of Colonel General;

General von Kleist, Commanding General of the Twenty-Second Army Corps, to the rank of Colonel General;

General Ritter von Schobert, Commanding General of the Seventh Army Corps, to the rank of Colonel General;

General Guderian, Commanding General of the Nineteenth Army Corps, to the rank of Colonel General;

General Hoth, Commanding General of the Fifteenth Army Corps, to the rank of Colonel General;

General Haase, Commanding General of the Third Army Corps, to the rank of Colonel General;

General Hoeppner, Commanding General of the Sixteenth Army Corps, to the rank of Colonel General;

General Fromm, Chief of Military Armament and Commander in Chief of the Replacement Army, to the rank of Colonel General.

In consideration of unequaled services rendered I promote:

Lieutenant General Dietl, Commanding General of the Mountain Corps in Norway, to the rank of Infantry General. As the first officer with the German Wehrmacht, I award him the Oak Leaves of the Knight's Cross of the Iron Cross.

Pending a later recognition of all the leaders and officers of the Reich Navy, I promote:

Admiral Carls, the Commanding Admiral of the Naval Station Baltic Sea and Commander in Chief of the Naval Troops East, to the rank of Admiral General.

In appreciation of the unequaled accomplishments of the German Luftwaffe,

I promote:

Colonel General Milch to the rank of Field Marshal;

General der Flieger Sperrle to the rank of Field Marshal;

General der Flieger Kesselring to the rank of Field Marshal.

I promote:

General der Flieger Stumpff to the rank of Colonel General;

General der Flieger Grauert to the rank of Colonel General;

General der Flieger Keller to the rank of Colonel General;

General of the Flak Artillery Weise to the rank of Colonel General;

General der Flieger Udet to the rank of Colonel General.

Furthermore,

I promote to the rank of General der Flieger:

Lieutenant General Geissler;
Major General Jeschonnek;
Lieutenant General Loerzer;
Lieutenant General Ritter von Greim;
and Major General Freiherr von Richthofen.

In my High Command of the Wehrmacht I promote:
Colonel General Keitel to the rank of Field Marshal;
Major General Jodl to the rank of Artillery General.

In announcing these promotions on the occasion of the most successful campaign in our history, before this forum and so before the entire nation, I thereby honor the entire Wehrmacht of the National Socialist Greater German Reich.

I cannot conclude my reflections on this battle without thinking of our ally here.

Ever since there has been a National Socialist regime, its foreign policy has embraced two goals:

1. Bringing about a true understanding and friendship with Italy and,
2. Bringing about the same relationship with England.

My Party Comrades, you know that I was as driven by these conceptions twenty years ago as I was later. I have dealt with and defended these ideas as a journalist and in my speeches countless times, as long as I myself was a mere opposition leader in the democratic republic.

I immediately undertook, as soon as the German people entrusted me with its leadership, to realize these oldest goals of National Socialist foreign policy in practical terms.

It still saddens me today that, in spite of all my endeavors, I have not succeeded in obtaining this friendship with England which, I believe, should have been a blessing for both peoples; and especially because I was not able to do so despite my persistent, sincere efforts.

However, I am all the more happy that at least the first point in this program of my foreign policy was in fact realized.

This I owe, above all, to the genius who today stands at the head of the Italian people. For it was possible only owing to his epoch-making activities for the two intellectually related revolutions to find each other, to finally seal in jointly-shed blood the alliance which is destined to procure a new life for Europe.

That I myself have the honor to be a friend of this man gladdens me all the more, in view of the unique story of his life, which bears evidence of as many similarities to my own as our two revolutions do to each other, and, beyond this, as does the history of the unification and rise of our two nations.

Ever since the resurrection of the German nation, we have heard many voices of understanding from Italy.

On the foundation of this mutual understanding grew a living community of interests. And finally this was set down in treaties. And when, last year, contrary to my expressed will and desire, this war was forced on the German Reich, a consultation on the further conduct of our two states involved Mussolini and myself.

The benefit derived for the Reich from the behavior of Italy was extraordinary. Not only economically did we profit from the situation and the stance of Italy, but also militarily.

From the beginning, Italy tied down strong forces of our enemies and curtailed above all their freedom of strategic disposition. And when the Duce determined that the time had come to take a stand with the weapon in his fist against the unbearable and persistent violation of Italy, damage done in particular by French and British transgression, and the King issued the declaration of war, then this was done with complete freedom of decision. All the greater must our gratitude be.

The intercession of Italy has sped up and assisted in opening France's eyes to the utter hopelessness of continued resistance.

And ever since, our ally has fought on the peaks and ridges of the Alps and now on the vast plains encompassed in his sphere of interest. Especially his present air attacks and battles at sea are being led with the spirit peculiar to the Fascist Revolution.

Here they elicit the spirit which binds National Socialism to Fascist Italy. Italy's pain is Germany's pain, as we have experienced in recent days in view of the death of Balbo. Its joy is our joy.

And our cooperation in the political and military fields is a complete one. It will erase the injustice done the German and

Italian peoples throughout the centuries. For, at the end of everything, stands the shared victory!

And when I now turn to speak of the future, my Deputies, I do so not to boast or brag. This I can well leave up to others who are in greater need of it, as for example Mr. Churchill. What I want to do is to paint a picture of the present situation, bare of exaggeration, as it is and as I see it.

1. The course of events in the ten months of war now lying behind us has proved my assessments correct and those of our adversaries incorrect:

When the British so-called statesmen assure us that their country emerges strengthened from every defeat and failure, then it surely is no arrogance when I inform them that we emerge at least equally strengthened from our successes.

On September 1 of the year now past, I already explained to you that, come what may, neither the force of weapons nor time shall force Germany to the ground. The Reich today stands stronger militarily than ever before.

We have seen the losses, individually surely heavy, though as a total relatively low, which the German Wehrmacht has suffered in battle within the past three months.

When you consider that, within this time, we erected a front which reaches from the North Cape to the Spanish border, then our losses are extraordinarily low, especially when compared with those of the World War.

The cause lies—besides with the, on an average, excellent leadership—with the outstanding tactical training of the individual soldier and of the units, as well as with the cooperation among the branches of the service.

Another cause is to be found with the quality and efficiency of the new weaponry.

A third cause lies with the conscious refusal to pursue what is called prestige. I myself have, on principle, labored to avoid any attack or operation which was not necessary in the context of the actual annihilation of the adversary, but was instead to be carried out for the sake of what was regarded as prestige.

In spite of all of this, naturally, we had anticipated far higher losses in many instances. The manpower saved will benefit us in the further pursuit of the struggle for freedom forced upon us.

At present, many of our divisions in France are being withdrawn and reassigned to their bases at home. Many men are able to take leaves of absence. Weaponry and equipment are being either repaired or replaced by new material. All in all, the Wehrmacht today is stronger than ever before.

2. Weaponry: The loss of weaponry in Norway, especially in the campaigns against Holland, Belgium, and France, is void of any significance.

It stands in no relation to production. Army and Luftwaffe possess at this moment—as I am speaking to you—equipment more complete and stronger than before we intervened in the West.

3. Ammunition: Provisions for ammunition were so well executed, the stocks are so vast, that in many areas production must now be curtailed or rerouted since the existing depots and warehouses, even given the greatest of efforts, in part are no longer capable of absorbing further deliveries. As in Poland, the consumption of ammunition was unexpectedly low. It stands in no relation to the stockpiles. The total reserves of the Army and the Luftwaffe are higher at present, for all categories of weapons, than before the attack in the West.

4. Raw materials essential to the war effort: Thanks to the Four-Year Plan,[32] Germany was prepared for the greatest of strains in an exemplary fashion. No armed forces in the world, other than Germany's Wehrmacht, have so benefited from a shift away from imported raw materials essential to the war effort to such as can be found within the country.

Thanks to the work of the Reichsmarschall, this transformation of the German economy into a war economy characterized by self-sufficiency was already achieved in peacetime.

---

[32] A series of economic reforms aimed at preparing Germany for self-sufficiency within four years, launched in 1936. The Four Year Plan sought to reduce unemployment, increase synthetic fiber production, undertake public works projects under the direction of Fritz Todt, increase automobile production, initiate numerous building and architectural projects, and further develop the Autobahn system.

We possess reserves of the two most important raw materials, coal and iron, in what I may well term an unlimited quantity. Fuel supplies are more than enough for consumption. The capacities of our production are increasing and, within a short time, they will suffice—even should imports cease—to satisfy demand completely.

Our advance metal collections have so increased our metal reserves that we can face a war of no matter what duration. We shall reign supreme no matter what happens.

Added to this are the enormous possibilities that come from a yet immeasurable bounty and including the development of the territories we have occupied.

Germany and Italy possess, within the confines of the area they regulate and control, an economic potential of about 200 million people, of whom only 130 million are soldiers, with seventy million free to be employed exclusively in different economic activities.[33]

I informed you on September 1, my Deputies, that for the further conduct of the war I had ordered the initial implementation of a new Five-Year Plan. I can now assure you that all measures to this end have been taken.

Come what may, I now no longer regard time as a threatening factor, not even in a general sense. This time, the measures taken in a timely fashion have also secured foodstuffs for a war of no matter how long a duration.

5. The attitude of the German nation: Thanks to National Socialist education, the German nation has not approached this war with the superficiality of a "hurrah" patriotism, but with the zealous determination of a race which knows the fate awaiting it should it suffer defeat.

The endeavors to subvert this unity, launched by the propaganda of our enemies, are as stupid as they are ineffective. Ten months of war have rendered this zealousness all the more

---

[33] A reference to the total population of the areas then under joint German and Italian control. Comprised of (approximate figures as of 1940) Germany, 69,838,000; Italy, 44,467,000; France, 40,690,000; Poland, 21,993,000; Netherlands, 8,923,000; Belgium, 8,100,000; Norway, 3,000,000; and Denmark, 3,832,000.

profound. And, in general, it is a great misfortune that the world's opinion is not formed by men who see things as they are, but by men who see them as they want them to be!

In the last days, I have seen through and studied countless documents from the Allied Headquarters.

Among other things, these contain reports on the atmosphere in Germany, or memoranda on the disposition and inner attitude of the German people.

The authors of these reports were, in part, also diplomats. Reading through these reports, one cannot help wondering whether their authors were blind, stupid, or simply vile scoundrels.

I will admit without further ado that, naturally, here in Germany also there have been, and perhaps still are today, certain individuals who have watched the Third Reich's conquests with a feeling akin to regret.

Incorrigible reactionaries or blind nihilists may well be saddened in their hearts that things came out not as they had willed them. But their numbers are ridiculously small and their significance is smaller yet.

Regrettably, this scum of the nation appears to have been chosen by the outside world as a measuring stick by which to assess the German nation. And from this, the sick minds of failed statesmen derive the last points of orientation to cling to for new hope.

As needed, the British warlords designate a "General Hunger" or an "imminent revolution" as their new allies. There is no nonsense that these people would not dish up for their own nation in order to cling to their positions for yet a few more weeks.

The German nation has proved, above all, its inner attitude through its sons who are fighting on the battlefield. Within weeks they have beaten Germany's strongest military adversary and have destroyed him. Their spirit was and remains the spirit of the German homeland.

6. The surrounding world: In the eyes of English politicians, their last hopes, besides those resting with the loyal and allied nations, lie with a series of propped-up heads of state without

thrones; statesmen without subjects; and generals without armies; as well as on renewed complications they believe they can conjure up thanks to their well-proven deftness in such matters.

A true Ahasuerus[34] amongst these hopes is the belief in a possible new estrangement to separate Germany and Russia. German-Russian relations have been established for good.

The reason for this was that England and France, with the support of certain smaller states, incessantly attributed to Germany ambitions to conquer terrain which lay completely outside the sphere of German interests.

Suddenly it was said, that Germany was eyeing the occupation of the Ukraine; then again it sought to invade Finland; at another time it was claimed that Romania was threatened; then finally even Turkey was endangered.

Given these circumstances, I held it to be proper to undertake, above all, with Russia, a sober delineation of interests, to once and for all clarify what Germany believes it must regard as its sphere of interest in securing its future, and what in turn Russia holds to be vital to its existence.

Based on this clear delineation of mutual spheres of interest, the Russo-German relationship was revised. It is childish to hope that in the course of this revision tensions might arise anew between Germany and Russia.

Germany has not stepped outside its sphere of interest, and neither has Russia.

England is deceived in its hope of bringing about a new European crisis to reprieve its own situation, insofar as the relationship of Germany to Russia is concerned.

Though the British statesmen are chronically slow in their comprehension of almost everything, they will surely come to understand this in the course of time.

I fancy that I correctly forecast the future development of this war in my speech of October 6. I assure you, my Deputies,

---

[34] From the thirteenth century "Wandering Jew" legend. The name of the Jew who, according to the legend, taunted Jesus on the way to the crucifixion and was then cursed to walk the earth until the Second Coming.

that not for a moment could I doubt victory. And, unless one feels the need to see signs and guarantees for the final victory exclusively in defeats, then I believe that the course of events up to this point has proved me right.

As I was certain of this course of events, I offered my hand to France and England at the time for an understanding.

You still recall the answer that I received.

My arguments against the nonsense of pursuing this war, on the certainty of gaining nothing, even under the most favorable of circumstances, and of losing much, were mocked and scoffed at, or passed over.

I promptly assured you then that I feared, because of my peace proposal, to be decried as a cockerel who no longer wants to fight because he is no longer able to fight. And this is exactly what happened.

I now believe that France—less the guilty statesmen than the people—thinks differently about this October 6 today. What nameless misery has befallen this great country and people since then.

I shall not even mention the toll of suffering the war has placed on their soldiers. For above this stands the suffering caused by the recklessness of those who drove millions of people from their homes without proper cause, who were compelled by the thought that this might somehow hamper the German war effort.

This premise defied comprehension: this evacuation was mostly to the detriment of the Allied war effort and, moreover, it was the cruelest experience for the unfortunate afflicted.

The injury the gentlemen Churchill and Reynaud have done millions of people, through their advice and commands—this they can neither justify in this world nor in the next.

All of this—as I said—need not have happened.

For peace was all I asked of France and England in October. But the gentlemen war profiteers wanted a continuation of this war at all cost. They have it now.

Still all I hear from London are cries—not the cries of the masses, but of the politicians—that this war must now, all the more, be pursued.

I do not know if these politicians have an inkling of just how this war is in fact to be pursued.

They declare that they will continue this war, and should England fall, then they will do so from Canada.

I do not believe this means that the English people will all emigrate to Canada, but rather that the gentlemen war profiteers will all retreat to Canada by themselves.

I fear the people will have to remain behind in England. And, assuredly, they will see the war with different eyes in London than their so-called leaders in Canada.

Believe me, my Deputies, I feel an inner disgust at this type of unscrupulous parliamentarian annihilators of peoples and states.

It is almost painful to me to have been chosen by Providence to give a shove to what these men have brought to the point of falling.

It was not my ambition to wage wars, but to build up a new social state of the highest culture. And every year of war takes me away from my work.

And the cause of this robbery is those ludicrous zeroes whom one could at best call nature's political run of the mill, insofar as their corrupted vileness does not brand them as something out of the ordinary.

Mr. Churchill has repeated the declaration that he wants war.

About six weeks ago now, he launched this war in an arena in which he apparently believes he is quite strong: namely, in the air war against the civilian population, albeit beneath the deceptive slogan of a so-called war against military objectives.

Ever since Freiburg, these objectives have turned out to be open cities, markets, villages, residential housing, hospitals, schools, kindergartens, and whatever else happens to be hit.

Up to now I have given little by way of response. This is not intended to signal, however, that this is the only response possible or that it shall remain this way!

I am fully aware that with our response, which one day will come, will also come the nameless suffering and misfortune of many men. Naturally, this does not apply to Mr. Churchill himself since by then he will surely be secure in Canada, where the money and the children of the most distinguished of war profiteers have already been brought. But there will be great tragedy for millions of other men.

And Mr. Churchill should make an exception and place trust in me when as a prophet I now proclaim: A great world empire will be destroyed. A world empire which I never had the ambition to destroy or as much as harm.

Alas, I am fully aware that the continuation of this war will end only in the complete shattering of one of the two warring parties. Mr. Churchill may believe this to be Germany. I know it to be England.

**In this hour I feel compelled, standing before my conscience, to direct yet another appeal to reason in England.**

**I believe I can do this as I am not asking for something as the vanquished, but rather, as the victor.**

**I am speaking in the name of reason.**

**I see no compelling reason which could force the continuation of this war.**

**I regret the sacrifices it will demand, I would like to spare my nation. I know the hearts of millions of men and boys glow at the thought of finally being allowed to wage battle against an enemy who has, without reasonable cause, declared war on us a second time.**

**But I also know of the women and mothers at home whose hearts, despite their willingness to sacrifice to the last, hang onto this last with all their might.**

**Mr. Churchill may well belittle my declaration again, crying that it was nothing other than a symptom of my fear, or my doubts of the final victory.**

**Still I will have an easy conscience in view of things to come.**

Deputies, Men of the German Reichstag.

In reflecting on the ten months lying behind us, all of us will surely feel overcome by the grace of Providence which allowed us to accomplish so great a task.

It has blessed our resolves and stood by us on many a difficult path. I myself am touched in recognition of the calling it imparted to me to restore freedom and honor to my nation. The disgrace we suffered for twenty-two years and which had its beginnings in the Forest of Compiègne was erased forever at the very same site.

Today I have named the men who, before history, enabled me to accomplish this great task. They have done their best, dedicating their talents and their industry to the German nation.

I now wish to conclude in mentioning all those nameless men who have no less done their duty.

Millions of them have risked life and liberty and, as brave German officers and soldiers, have been ready at every hour to make the last sacrifice a man can make.

Today many of them rest in the same graves in which their fathers have rested since the Great War.

They bear evidence to silent heroism. They stand as a symbol for all those hundreds of thousands of musketeers, anti-tank gunners and tank gunners, pioneers and artillerymen, soldiers of the Navy and the Luftwaffe, men of the Waffen SS, and all those other fighters who stood for the German Wehrmacht in the struggle for the freedom and future of our Nation and for the eternal greatness of the National Socialist Greater German Reich.

Germany—Hail Victory!

# Part III: Hitler's Political Testament, Berlin, April 29, 1945

## Section 1: Introduction

On April 29, 1945, Hitler calmly dictated a private and a political last will and testament. The private will discussed personal matters with regard to his possessions and family, and the political will was meant to be a last political statement.

Hitler used this document—his last ever public statement—to once again point out that he had tried everything possible to avoid the war.

Three copies of the testaments were smuggled out of the already besieged Reichs Chancellery area of Berlin. They were given to three trusted men: deputy press attaché, Heinz Lorenz; Hitler's army adjutant Willy Johannmeyer, and Martin Bormann's adjutant SS-Standartenführer Wilhelm Zander. All three escaped from Berlin, and were apprehended by British or American forces.

The testaments ended up being preserved in British and US archives, but were released to the general public in 1946.

## Section 2: Hitler's Political Testament

My Political Testament

More than thirty years have now passed since 1914 when I made my modest contribution as a volunteer in the first world war, which was forced upon the Reich.

In these three decades, my life and all my thoughts and deeds have been motivated solely by my love for and loyalty to my people. They gave me the strength to make the most difficult decisions that have ever confronted mortal man. In these three

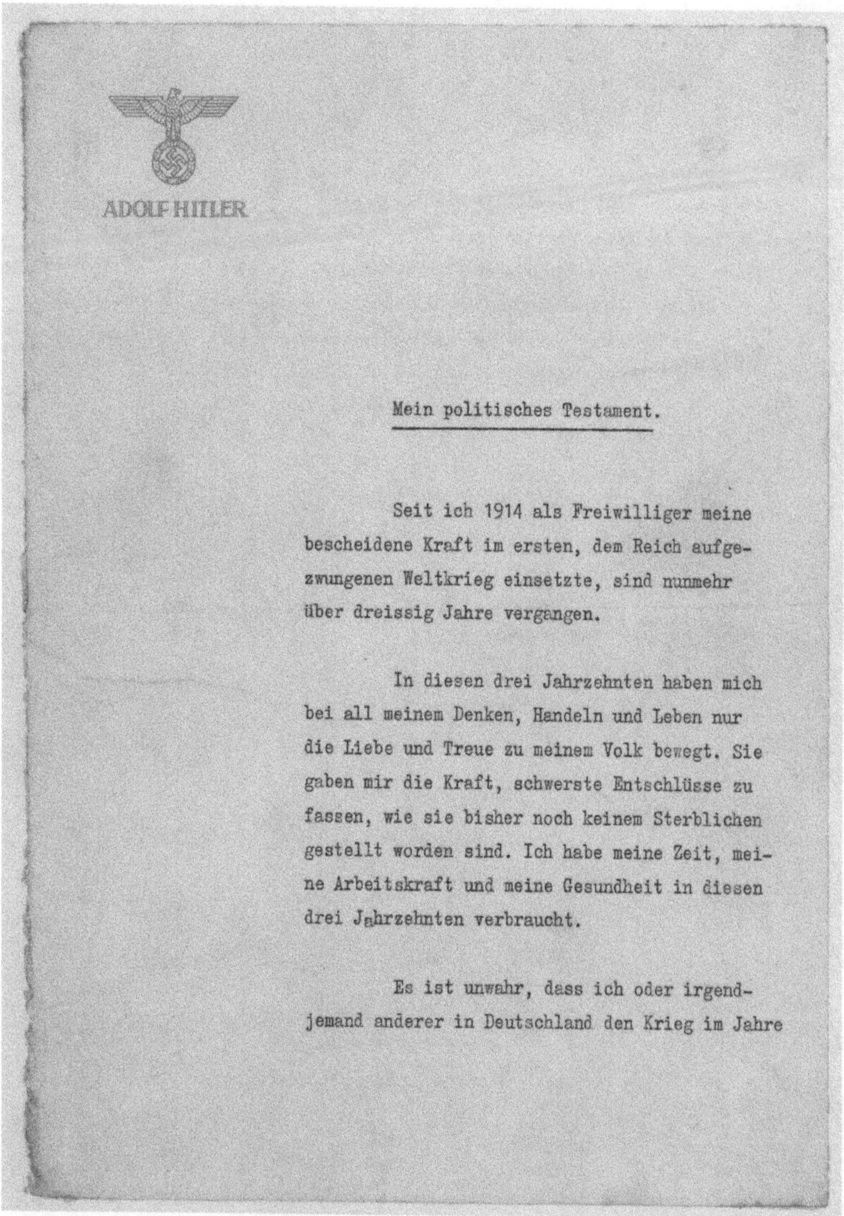

ADOLF HITLER

Mein politisches Testament.

Seit ich 1914 als Freiwilliger meine bescheidene Kraft im ersten, dem Reich aufgezwungenen Weltkrieg einsetzte, sind nunmehr über dreissig Jahre vergangen.

In diesen drei Jahrzehnten haben mich bei all meinem Denken, Handeln und Leben nur die Liebe und Treue zu meinem Volk bewegt. Sie gaben mir die Kraft, schwerste Entschlüsse zu fassen, wie sie bisher noch keinem Sterblichen gestellt worden sind. Ich habe meine Zeit, meine Arbeitskraft und meine Gesundheit in diesen drei Jahrzehnten verbraucht.

Es ist unwahr, dass ich oder irgendjemand anderer in Deutschland den Krieg im Jahre

***The first page of Hitler's original Political Testament, held in the US National Archives.***

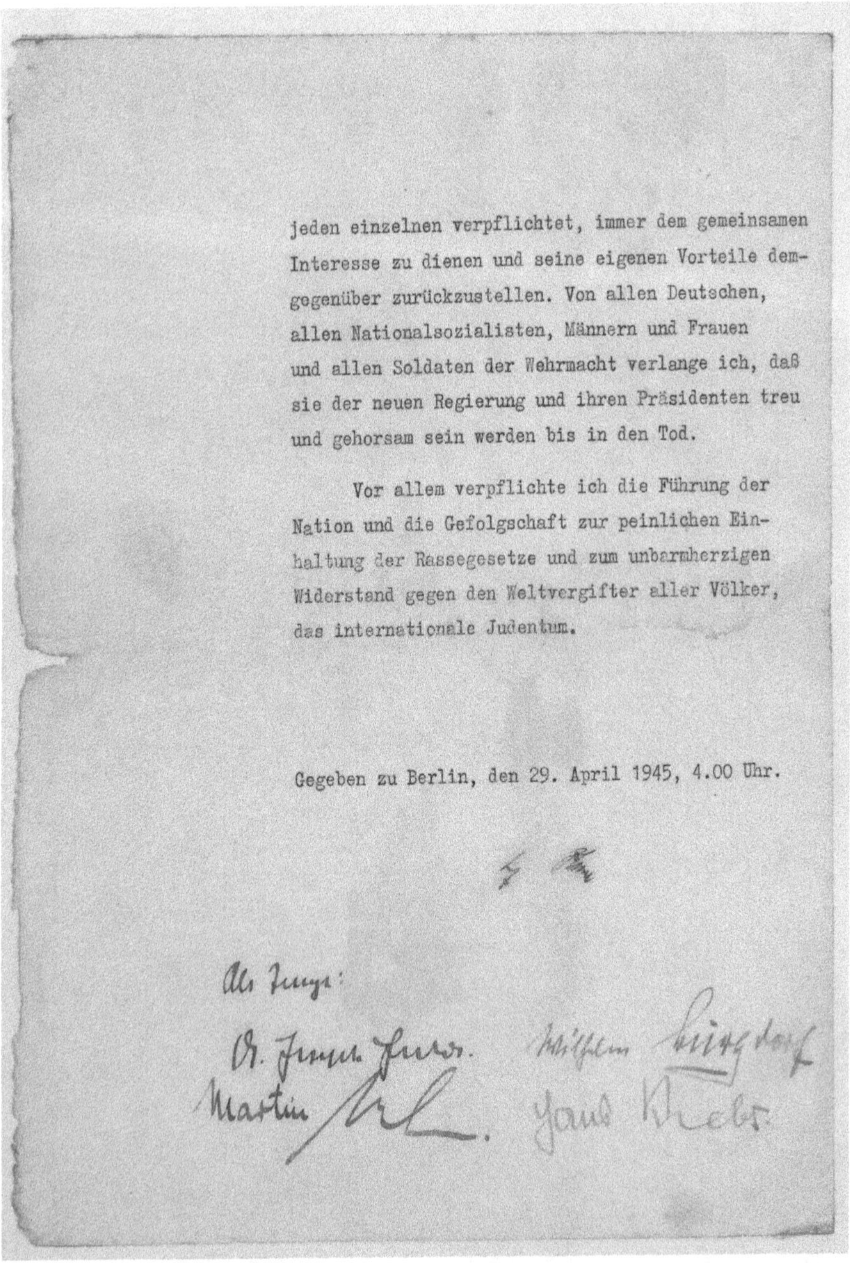

jeden einzelnen verpflichtet, immer dem gemeinsamen Interesse zu dienen und seine eigenen Vorteile demgegenüber zurückzustellen. Von allen Deutschen, allen Nationalsozialisten, Männern und Frauen und allen Soldaten der Wehrmacht verlange ich, daß sie der neuen Regierung und ihren Präsidenten treu und gehorsam sein werden bis in den Tod.

Vor allem verpflichte ich die Führung der Nation und die Gefolgschaft zur peinlichen Einhaltung der Rassegesetze und zum unbarmherzigen Widerstand gegen den Weltvergifter aller Völker, das internationale Judentum.

Gegeben zu Berlin, den 29. April 1945, 4.00 Uhr.

Als Zeuge:

***The last page of Hitler's original Political Testament, held in the US National Archives.***

decades I have exhausted my time, my working strength, and my health.

It is not true that I or anyone else in Germany wanted the war in 1939. It was desired and instigated exclusively by those international statesmen who were either of Jewish origin or who worked for Jewish interests.

I have made too many offers for the control and limitation of armaments, which posterity will not be able to disregard forever—for the responsibility for the outbreak of this war to be laid on me. I have furthermore never wished that after the first disastrous world war a second should arise against England, much less against America.

Centuries will pass away, but out of the ruins of our cities and monuments the hatred will continually grow anew against the people that is ultimately responsible, and for whom we have to thank for all this: international Jewry and its helpers!

Three days before the outbreak of the German-Polish war I again proposed to the British ambassador in Berlin a solution to the German-Polish problem—one similar to the solution that had been applied in the case of the Saar territory involving international supervision. That proposal likewise cannot be denied.

It was rejected only because the leading circles in English politics wanted the war, partly on account of the hoped-for business opportunities, and partly prompted by the propaganda organized by international Jewry.

I have also left no doubt that, if the nations of Europe were once again to be treated as mere objects of commerce, to be bought and sold by these international conspirators in money and finance, then the people that is really guilty of this murderous conflict will also be held accountable: Jewry!

Moreover, I left no one in doubt that this time millions of European children of the Aryan nations were not going to starve, and millions of grown men were not going to suffer death, and hundreds of thousands of women and children were not going to be burned and bombed to death in cities, without the real guilty ones having to atone for their guilt, even if by more humane means.

After six years of war, which in spite of all setbacks will ultimately will go down in history as the most glorious and valiant expression of a nation's will to life, I cannot forsake the city that is the capital of this Reich.

Given that the forces are not sufficient to hold out any longer against the enemy offensive here, and that our own resistance is gradually being weakened by men who are as deluded as they are lacking in initiative, I wish, by remaining in this city, to share my fate with those millions of others who have also accepted to do so.

Moreover I do not wish to fall into the hands of an enemy who requires a new spectacle organized by the Jews for the amusement of their incited masses.

I have therefore decided to remain in Berlin and here of my own free will to choose death at the moment when I believe the headquarters of the Führer and Chancellor itself can no longer be held. I die with a joyful heart, mindful of the immeasurable deeds and achievements of our soldiers at the front, our women at home, the achievements of our farmers and workers, and the efforts, unique in history, of our youth that bears my name.

That I express my thanks to you all from the bottom of my heart is just as self-evident as my wish that you should therefore on no account give up the struggle, but rather continue it against the enemies of the Fatherland, no matter where, true to the principles of the great Clausewitz.

From the sacrifice of our soldiers and from my own solidarity with them unto death, will in any case arise from German history the seed of a radiant renaissance of the National Socialist movement and thereby of the realization of a true national community.

Many of the most courageous men and women have decided at the end to unite their lives with mine. I have begged and finally ordered them not to do that, but instead to take part in the further struggle of the nation.

I beg the leaders of the armies, the navy and the air force to strengthen by all possible means the spirit of resistance of our soldiers in the National Socialist spirit, with special reference to the fact that I myself, as founder and creator of this movement, have also preferred death to cowardly abdication or even capitulation.

May it, at some future time, become a matter of honor for the German officer— as is already the case in our navy—that the surrender of a district or of a town is impossible, and that these leaders especially here must go forward as shining examples, faithfully fulfilling their duty unto death.

(List of appointments to the new cabinet, and expulsions from the party follow).

Above all I enjoin the leaders of the nation and their followers to scrupulous observance of the laws of race, and to merciless resistance to the universal poisoner of all peoples, international Jewry.

Berlin, April 29, 1945, 4:00 a.m.
Adolf Hitler
Witnesses
Dr. Joseph Goebbels
Wilhelm Burgdorf
Martin Bormann
Hans Krebs

# Part IV: Last Letter from Hermann Göring to Winston Churchill, Nuremberg, October 15, 1946.

## Section 1: Introduction.

Hermann Göring was not only head of the Luftwaffe, or German Air Force, but president of the Reichstag, and, until April 29, 1945, officially Hitler's deputy.

Although removed from that position in Hitler's political testament, Göring knew that this act had been committed in error caused by the confusion and desperation of the time, and remained steadfastly loyal to his Führer to the end.

When asked by the Nuremberg Court to renounce Hitler, he refused, saying he had stood by Hitler in good times and would continue to do so in bad, adding that it was his single greatest source of sorrow to think that Hitler had thought that he (Göring) had betrayed him in his final hours.

Göring also explained to the Court that the reason why he had agreed to surrender was so that someone would speak for Germany in whatever was to follow the collapse.

He was well aware that the Allies would seek his execution, and only took part in the proceedings to make his point—which he did effectively, scoring many points off the prosecution and valiantly defending Germany and the Third Reich against many of the allegations—later proven to be lies—which were made at the trial proceedings.

Sentenced to death for "waging aggressive war"—by a court which had as judges representatives of the Soviet Union, which had been Germany's ally for the first two years of the war and who had themselves invaded Poland, Finland, Estonia, Latvia and Lithuania—Göring determined that he would take his own life rather than be hanged. Thus, on October 15, 1946, just a few hours before his scheduled execution, Göring took cyanide—but not before writing several letters, including the one reproduced below, addressed to Winston Churchill in person.

## Section 2: Last Letter from Hermann Göring to Winston Churchill

Mr. Churchill,

You will have the satisfaction to survive me and my comrades in misfortune. I do not hesitate to congratulate you on this personal triumph and the finesse with which you have accomplished it. You have gone to great expense in order to secure this success, for yourself and Great Britain.

Should I believe you sufficiently naive as to consider this success anything more than a show, detrimental to the Great German Empire, a performance for the peoples and their Jewish and Bolshevist confederates which were maneuvered by you into the war, then my statement to you during the last hour of my life would also in the eyes of posterity be squandered upon an undeserving one.

My pride as a German and as one of the foremost responsible German leaders forbids me to lose even a single word in a dispute of world-historical importance on the disgraceful lowliness of the methods employed by the victors as far as these proceedings concern my own person.[35]

However, as it is the obvious and announced intention of their administration of the law to throw the very German people into the abyss of illegality and to rob them once and for all of a future possibility to defend themselves by the removal of the responsible men of the National Socialist state, I have to add a few words to the historic subject of the verdict, premeditated by you and your allies.

---

[35] A reference to the legally-flawed Nuremberg Trials, of which Field Marshall Bernard Montgomery was later to say that he never wanted to lead an army again, because it had now "become a crime to lose a war."

I direct these remarks to you, since you are one of the best informed ones regarding the true underlying reasons for this war and the possibility of avoiding the same; in at least a manner bearable to the European future; and yet refused your testimony and your oath to your own high court of justice.

Therefore, I shall not fail, while there is still time, to call you before the tribunal of history and direct my statements to you, because I know that this tribunal will expose you some day as that man, who with ambition, intelligence and energy has thrown the fate of the European nations under the heels of foreign world powers.

In you I identify before history the man who had the ability to bring Adolf Hitler down and his political accomplishments; the man who will, however, be unable to raise the shield protectively against the invasion of Europe by the Asiatics.

It was your ambition to justify the Versailles Treaty regarding Germany.

It will prove fatal to you that you succeeded. You personified the hardened obstinacy of your old gentry; and you also personified the stubbornness of its old age, opposing the last gigantic effort of the rejuvenated German power to decide the fate of Europe in the steppes of Asia in order to safeguard the same in the future.

Long after my responsibility in the future development of events has found its objective judge, it will be put to your account that the past bloody war has not been the final one which had to be fought on the Continent for the very possibility of the existence of its nations.

You will have to answer for the fact that the bloody war of yesterday will be followed by a still greater one and that the European nations will not rule at the Volga, but at the Pyrenees mountains.

It is my fervent wish that you may at least live to see the day on which the world, and the western nations in particular, will become aware of the bitter truth that it was you and your friend Roosevelt who sold the future to Bolshevism for a cheap personal triumph over nationalistic Germany. This day may come sooner than you like, and you in spite of your advanced age, will be vigorous enough to see it dawn bloody red over the British Isles.

I am convinced that it will bring you all those unimaginable terrors which you escaped this time through the good luck of war; or through the abhorrence of the German conduct of war to a complete degeneration of the methods of fighting of peoples of the same Race.

My knowledge regarding the kind and amount of arms and of projects from us, which—thanks to your military assistance to the Red Army—have fallen into their hands, enable me to form this supposition.

There is no doubt that you—according to your habit—soon will write good memoirs and you will write them the better, as there is nobody to hinder you to tell and suppress what you like.

You believe it very clever to have submitted this historic truth to the craftiness to a handful of ambitious junior lawyers in

***Hermann Göring addresses the Nuremberg Court.***

order to have it changed into an expedient dialectic treatise, in spite of your awareness as a Briton as well as a statesmen, that with such means the problems of existence of peoples could not be solved and judged; neither in the past nor in the future.

I have an only too well grounded opinion of your power and the cunning of your intelligence to credit you with believing the vulgar propaganda with which you motivated the war against us and with which you have had your victory over us glorified in a fantastic show.

I state here with great emphasis as one of the highest military, political and economic leaders of the Great German Empire the following:

This war could not be avoided because the politics of Great Britain— under the influence of your person and of your friends of like opinions in all fields— persisted constantly to hinder the life interests and the most natural development of the German people; and—filled with the senile ambition to uphold the British hegemony—preferred the Second World War to an understanding, as we on our side had tried time and again to bring about, beneficial to both of the most prominent nations of Europe.

I declare herewith once more and most emphatically that the guilt of the German people in this war— into which they were forced by you—consists solely in trying to end the eternal difficulties to their national existence, which you artfully instigated and continued.

It would be useless to go with you into any dispute over the causes, the conditions of restraint and the motives which led during the course of the war to the political and military complications and which your lawyers knew so well to use in a one-sided manner at the cost of the National Socialist regime.

The devastated regions of the European culture and robbed treasures give still today testimony of your embittered despair with which a great and proud people yesterday, with unparalleled readiness to make sacrifices fought for its existence.

Tomorrow they will testify that alone the overpowering might, led by you in the field, was able to cause the subjection and deprivation of their rights. The day after tomorrow the

Russians will bear witness to the betrayal, which surrendered Europe to the red Asiatics.

The Germany which you conquered will take revenge on you through its downfall. You have neither produced a better politic nor shown a greater courage than we.

You have not won the victory due to better qualities or superiority of your strength or strategy, but merely after six years with the predominance of your allies.

Do not believe your victory to be all that which you tell the world. You and your hand will soon harvest the fruits of your political art.

What you as an experienced Cynic will not admit toward us—namely that our fight in the East was an act of urgent self-defense, and not alone for Germany but for all of Europe; and that the Germans fighting this war; which you constantly condemned, therefore was justified. This, your ally and friend of today, Stalin, will soon prove to you and the British Empire.

Then you will experience what it means to fight this enemy and you will learn that necessity knows no law; also that you can neither fight him successfully with treaties in law nor with the weight of Great Britain and her European dwarfs.

You have stated to the German people that you were primarily concerned with the restoration of their democratic mode of life.

But you have not said a single word that you want to restore to them the sensible foundations of living, which have been denied to them these past 25 years.

Your name stands under all essential documents of this epoch of British want of comprehension and jealousy towards Germany.

Your name will also stand under the result with which this epoch of Germany's liquidation has challenged history in lieu of Europe's existence.

My belief in the vitality of my people cannot be shaken. They will be stronger and live longer than you.

However, it distresses me to know that defenseless in your power, they now also belong to the luckless victims, who thanks to your success, do not approach a future of progressive work for the realization of their common aim, set forth by intelligence for the western peoples, but are driven towards the greatest catastrophe in their common history.

I do not wish to argue about outrages, which you rightly or wrongly ascribe to us and which neither agree with nor the German peoples comprehension; neither do I wish to talk about those atrocities which have been committed on your part and on the part of your allies towards millions of Germans; for I know that you have made under this pretext the entire German people the object of a collective outrage of a proportion never known in history.

I also know that you would not have acted differently regarding your treatment of Germany without this pretence, because since 1914 you have striven for nothing less than the destruction of the German empire.

This, your historic goal denies you the office of a judge over the avoidable and unavoidable consequences caused by your

***Göring and Alfred Rosenberg, Reich Ministry for the Occupied Eastern Territories, at Nuremberg.***

unremitting intentions and which were welcome to you as subsequent proof for the justification of your actions.

Today I regret my and the National Socialist Government's greatest mistake, the fateful error to believe in your discernment as a statesman.

I regret to have trusted you with justifiability recognizing the world-political necessity of a peaceful and progressive (prosperous) Germany for the existence of a flourishing England.

I regret that our means did not suffice to convince you at the last moment that the liquidation of Germany would also be the beginning of the liquidation of Britain's world power.

We began to act—each one according to his own law, I in line with the new one, for which this Europe was already too old—you holding on to the old one, for which this Europe is no longer anymore important enough in the world.

I shall know how to approach my end in the absolute conviction as a German National Socialist and considering everything else, to have been a better European than you.

I leave the judgment of this with an easy mind to posterity.

I hope sincerely that you will belong to this world for a long time to come as fate might grant you—as it has to me—when you decline to leave the posterity also a truth.

Herman Göring.

# Part V: "The World Jews Have Forced England into the War"—Neville Chamberlain in *The Forrestal Diaries*

## Section 1: Introduction

James Vincent Forrestal (1892–1949) was appointed as the United States Secretary of the Navy by Franklin D. Roosevelt in 1944, and served in that position until 1947, when he was appointed as the first United States Secretary of Defense. He held this position until he was forced to resign in 1949.

He died later the same year after falling to his death out of a window at the National Naval Medical Center (NNMC) in Bethesda, Maryland.

His diaries from 1944 to March 1949 were serialized in the *New York Herald Tribune* in 1951, and published as a 581 page book, *The Forrestal Diaries,* in October 1951.

Although they were censored prior to publication, certain fascinating details slipped through—dealing with the origin of the Second World War.

One of these was contained in an entry of a conversation he had with Joseph P. Kennedy (father of the later president John F. Kennedy), who had served as Roosevelt's ambassador in Berlin prior to the outbreak of the war.

## Section 2: Neville Chamberlain—"The World Jews Have Forced England into the War"

Forrestal's diary entry of his conversation with Joseph P. Kennedy reads as follows:

I asked him [Kennedy] about his conversations with Roosevelt and Neville Chamberlain from 1938 on. He said Chamberlain's position in 1938 was that English had nothing with which to fight and that she could not risk going to war with Hitler.

Kennedy's view: that Hitler would have fought Russia without any later conflict with England if it had not been for Bullitt's [William C. Bullitt, then ambassador to France] urging on Roosevelt in the summer of 1939 that the Germans must be faced down about Poland; neither the French nor the British would have made Poland a case of war if it had not been for the constant needling from Washington.

Bullitt, he said, kept telling Roosevelt that the Germans wouldn't fight. Kennedy said they would, and that they would overrun Europe.

Chamberlain, he said, stated that America and the world Jews had forced England into the war.

# THE FORRESTAL DIARIES

## HIS PRIVATE RECORDS, A MYSTERY UNTIL NOW, CAST A NEW LIGHT ON WARTIME WASHINGTON AND THE DEFENSE SECRETARY WHO PLAYED A BRILLIANT, CONTROVERSIAL ROLE IN ITS EVENTS

**When the executors of the estate of James Forrestal released his personal diaries, the New York *Herald Tribune*'s Walter Millis, assisted by Eugene Duffield, Forrestal's former aide, spent six painstaking months editing and annotating them into the form in which they are currently appearing in the *Tribune*. In the same form they will appear Oct. 11 as a book (the Viking Press, $5). The following article on *The Forrestal Diaries* has been written by LIFE Staff Writer Ernest Havemann, author of LIFE's close-up of the late Defense Secretary (LIFE, Oct. 6, 1947). All material quoted from the diaries is copyrighted, 1951, by the New York Herald Tribune, Inc.**

James V. Forrestal, the most brilliant U.S. public official of the last quarter century, had two great tragedies in his career. The first was his shyness, which rendered him unable to go on public exhibition and confined the influence of his magnificent logic to a narrow circle of intimates. The second, which possibly grew out of the first, was his suicide in 1949—at a time when he was only 57 and his nation, just beginning to realize the terrible urgency of the cold war, probably needed him more than ever before. Because of these two tragedies a certain air of mystery has hung over Forrestal. During his lifetime, since he was so loath to express himself in public, he was widely misunderstood. The "liberals" got on him in the days when it was popular to love Joe Stalin—and, for some reason which only a scholar of mass psychology could hope to fathom, stayed on him long after the myth of Russian sweetness and light had been exposed. (This whole phenomenon baffled Forrestal. In 1944 he wrote to a friend, "I find that whenever any American suggests that we act in accordance with the needs of our own security he is apt to be called a god-damned fascist or imperialist, while if Uncle Joe suggests that he needs the Baltic Provinces, half of Poland, all of Bessarabia and access to the Mediterranean, all hands agree that he is a fine, frank, candid and generally delightful fellow who is very easy to deal with because he is so explicit in what he wants.") After his suicide the Forrestal legend took on another shadowy dimension. As Shakespeare so well established, the misfortunes of great men have an eerie fascination, not unmixed with satisfaction and triumph, for those who have been unable to rise quite so high.

When it became known after Forrestal's death that he had left behind him a set of diaries, so secret that he insisted they be locked up in the White House, these documents immediately became the subject of intense speculation. This fall, uncensored except for security reasons, full of sharp and often embarrassing observations about many Washington characters and events since 1944, they are finally being published—in serial form by the New York *Herald Tribune* and in book form by the Viking Press. The diaries do not shed any light on the Forrestal suicide; the last page is dated more than two months before his death, and nothing except possibly a decrease in the number of entries toward the end shows any sign of nervous collapse or despair. The diaries do, however, tell a great deal about the life, the ideas and the brilliance of James Forrestal. Jotted down informally and with utter frankness, they are one of the future historian's best sources for the lowdown on the U.S. 1940s.

There is, for example, the entry of Dec. 27, 1945, which gets to the heart of a debate that has raged and will still rage, just beneath the surface if not quite on it, over the role of Franklin Roosevelt in the origin of and the U.S. entry in World War II. On that day exercise-loving Forrestal played golf with Joseph P. Kennedy, the anti-Roosevelt man who by an irony of fate was Roosevelt's ambassador to Britain before the war. Kennedy's views about the war are well known to students of that period, but they have never been reported so succinctly as by Forrestal:

> I asked him [Kennedy] about his conversations with Roosevelt and Neville Chamberlain from 1938 on. He said Chamberlain's position in 1938 was that England had nothing with which to fight and that she could not risk going to war with Hitler. Kennedy's view: that Hitler would have fought Russia without any later conflict with England if it had not been for Bullitt's [William C. Bullitt, then ambassador to France] urging on Roosevelt in the summer of 1939 that the Germans must be faced down about Poland; neither the French nor the British would have made Poland a cause of war if it had not been for the constant needling from Washington. Bullitt, he said, kept telling Roosevelt that the Germans wouldn't fight. Kennedy that they would, and that they would overrun Europe. Chamberlain, he says, stated that America and the world Jews had forced England into the war. In his telephone conversation with Roosevelt in the summer of 1939 the President kept telling him to put some iron up Chamberlain's backside. Kennedy's response always was that putting iron up his backside did no good unless the British had some iron with which to fight, and they did not. . . .

The Kennedy view was the extreme one; he was one of the most unrelenting of the hands-off isolationists. The Forrestal dissection of the Kennedy argument, as entered in the diary immediately following this paragraph, is therefore of even more interest:

> Looking backward there is undoubtedly foundation for Kennedy's belief that Hitler's attack could have been deflected to Russia, but I think he fails to take into account what would have happened after Hitler had conquered Russia. Would he have been content to stop? Nothing in his record indicates that that would have been the case, but rather that, having removed the threat to his eastern frontiers, he would then have exercised the options open to him to construct a European German-dominated system to which he later gave expression after overrunning France.
>
> The fundamental difficulty of England, however, was that if they backed Germany . . . they were then faced with a greater Germany, a weakened France and a relatively defenseless England, whereas an alliance with Russia and the ultimate destruction of Germany would present England with precisely the problem that they now have, namely, a vacuum of power in Central Europe into which Russian influence would flow.

Forrestal had a genius, as many entries of this type in the diaries show, for reducing a complicated world problem to its simplest essentials—and yet of avoiding any speciously simple or one-sided opinion. He never especially admired the foreign policies of Franklin Roosevelt. But neither did he, as that 1945 entry shows, go along with the shallow viewpoint of the Kennedys. To Forrestal most of the world's problems were dilemmas which became even sharper and more difficult of solution as they became more clearly understood. Some of his associates in Washington often wished that he were a little faster to make up his mind and take a firm position. The diaries now show what his real intimates knew even then—that his hesitation was usually the fear of an intellectual angel to tread where fools are far too prone to rush in.

As the Kennedy entry also indicates, Forrestal was a keen student of people. A known anti-New Dealer in a New Deal administration, he had the opportunity of associating with men on all sides of the political fences, listening to their arguments, watching them in action and reaching his own conclusions about their abilities and instincts. He had certain prejudices—for example, he viewed Henry Wallace with the unbelieving curiosity one might have for a man from Mars—but usually his judgments were a model of objectivity, which was a habit of mind reinforced by his early training as a newspaper reporter. His observations of President Truman are perhaps the most interesting of all.

◀—THIS WAS FORRESTAL, FIRST U.S. SECRETARY OF DEFENSE, IN 1947

CONTINUED ON NEXT PAGE 77

**Life Magazine, *October 15, 1951, with the quotation from Chamberlain claiming that the "world Jews" had forced Britain into the war.***

## Section 3: Forrestal and His Own Comments on the Jewish Lobby

Forrestal was no stranger to controversy with Jews. During private cabinet meetings with President Harry S. Truman in 1946 and 1947, Forrestal argued strongly against the then proposed partition of Palestine on the grounds it would infuriate Arab countries who supplied oil to the US.[1]

When news of Forrestal's opposition to the Zionist plan to seize Palestine became public, Truman received written threats to cut off campaign contributions from wealthy Jewish donors, as well as hate mail, including a letter accusing him of "preferring fascist and Arab elements to the democracy-loving Jewish people of Palestine."[2]

Forrestal complained of the power of the Jewish lobby to J. Howard McGrath, Senator from Rhode Island, and recorded it in his diary as follows: "...no group in this country should be permitted to influence our policy to the point it could endanger our national security."

It was little wonder that he was soon dismissed from office.

---

1 Donovan, Robert J. (1996). *Conflict and Crisis: The Presidency of Harry S. Truman, 1945–1948,* University of Missouri Press, p. 325–335.

2 *Ibid,* p. 325, "Visibly upset, Truman gave the letter to an aide, stating that he was far too angry to answer it in a polite manner."

CPSIA information can be obtained
at www.ICGtesting.com
Printed in the USA
BVHW081923180719
553810BV00002B/146/P

9 781684 186105